ECONOMIC ISSUES, PROBLEMS AND PERSPECTIVES

UNITED STATES FEDERAL BUDGET PROCESS

ECONOMIC ISSUES, PROBLEMS AND PERSPECTIVES

Additional books in this series can be found on Nova's website under the Series tab.

Additional E-books in this series can be found on Nova's website under the E-books tab.

AMERICAN POLITICAL, ECONOMIC, AND SECURITY ISSUES

Additional books in this series can be found on Nova's website under the Series tab.

Additional E-books in this series can be found on Nova's website under the E-books tab.

ECONOMIC ISSUES, PROBLEMS AND PERSPECTIVES

UNITED STATES FEDERAL BUDGET PROCESS

GERARD T. BRENNER
AND
ALEXANDER K. MONROE
EDITORS

Nova Science Publishers, Inc.
New York

For permission to use material from this book please contact us:
Telephone 631-231-7269; Fax 631-231-8175
Web Site: http://www.novapublishers.com

LIBRARY OF CONGRESS CATALOGING-IN-PUBLICATION DATA

United States federal budget process / editors, Gerard T. Brenner and
Alexander K. Monroe.
p. cm.
Includes index.
ISBN 978-1-61209-844-9 (hbk.)
1. Budget--United States. 2. Government spending policy--United States.
3. United States--Appropriations and expenditures. 4. United
States--Economic policy--2009- I. Brenner, Gerard T. II. Monroe, Alexander
K.
HJ2051.U545 2011
352.4'80973--dc22
2011004976

Published by Nova Science Publishers, Inc. † New York

CONTENTS

PREFACE

Budgeting for the federal government is an enormously complex process. It entails dozens of subprocesses, countless rules and procedures, the efforts of tens of thousands of staff persons in the executive and legislative branches, millions of work hours each year and the active participation of the President and congressional leaders, as well as other Members of Congress and executive officials. This new book examines the points of order in the congressional budget process; baselines and scorekeeping; allocations and subdivisions; entitlements and appropriated entitlements; basic federal budgeting terminology; federal budget process reform in the 111th Congress and FY2011 budget proposals and projections.

Chapter 1- Budgeting for the federal government is an enormously complex process. It entails dozens of subprocesses, countless rules and procedures, the efforts of tens of thousands of staff persons in the executive and legislative branches, millions of work hours each year, and the active participation of the President and congressional leaders, as well as other Members of Congress and executive officials.

Chapter 2- The Congressional Budget Act of 1974 (Titles I-IX of P.L. 93-344, as amended) created a process that Congress uses each year to establish and enforce the parameters for budgetary legislation. Enforcement of budgetary decisions is accomplished through the use of points of order, and through the reconciliation process. Points of order are prohibitions against certain types of legislation or congressional actions. These prohibitions are enforced when a Member raises a point of order against legislation that may violate these rules when it is considered by the House or Senate.

Chapter 3- Baselines and scorekeeping are an integral part of the federal budget process, providing lawmakers with a framework for making and enforcing budgetary decisions. The existing-law baseline, currently used by Congress, is a projection of federal spending, revenue, and the deficit (or surplus) that would occur if existing law were left unchanged. The baseline serves as a benchmark for federal budget decisions. Scorekeeping is the process by which the budgetary impact of proposed and enacted budget policies is measured; it assists Congress in making and enforcing budgetary decisions. This chapter provides a brief explanation of baselines and scorekeeping and their uses in the federal budget process.

Chapter 4- The annual budget resolution sets forth total spending and revenue levels for at least five fiscal years. The spending amounts are allocated, or "crosswalked," to the House and Senate committees having jurisdiction over discretionary spending (the Appropriations Committees) and direct spending (the legislative committees). The committee allocations provide Congress with one means of enforcing the spending levels of a budget resolution after it has been adopted.

Chapter 5- Entitlements are programs that require payments to persons, state or local governments, or other entities if specific eligibility criteria established in the authorizing law are met. Entitlement payments are legal obligations of the federal government, and eligible beneficiaries may have legal recourse if full payment under the law is not provided. This chapter provides a brief explanation of spending for entitlements, including so-called appropriated entitlements, and discusses the procedural and statutory constraints on legislation affecting such entitlement spending.

Chapter 6- In its most elemental form, the federal budget is a comprehensive accounting of the government's spending, revenues, and borrowing. This chapter provides a brief overview of the basic terminology and concepts used in the federal budget process.

Chapter 7- Procedural change is a recurrent feature of federal budgeting, although the scope and impact of changes may vary from year to year. In order to advance their budgetary, economic, or political objectives, both Congress and the President regularly propose and make changes to the federal budget process. This chapter briefly discusses the context in which federal budget process changes are made and identifies selected reform proposals by major category. The identification of reform proposals in this chapter is not intended to be comprehensive.

Chapter 8- While considering the FY20 11 budget, Congress faces very large budget deficits, rising costs of entitlement programs, and significant spending on overseas military operations. In FY2008 and FY2009, the enactment of financial intervention and fiscal stimulus legislation helped to bolster the economy, though it increased the deficit. While GDP growth has returned in recent quarters, unemployment remains elevated and government spending on "automatic stabilizer" programs, such as unemployment insurance and income support, remains higher than historical averages.

Chapter 9- This chapter provides an overview of major budget estimates and projections for the FY20 11 federal budget cycle. The report presents and compares budget projections calculated by the Obama Administration's Office of Management and Budget (OMB) and the Congressional Budget Office (CBO). In addition, the report discusses major budgetary issues.

In: United States Federal Budget Process
Editors: Gerard T. Brenner et al.
ISBN: 978-1-61209-844-9

Chapter 1

INTRODUCTION TO THE FEDERAL BUDGET PROCESS

Bill Heniff Jr., Sandy Streeter, Megan Suzanne Lynch and Jessica Tollestrup

SUMMARY

Budgeting for the federal government is an enormously complex process. It entails dozens of subprocesses, countless rules and procedures, the efforts of tens of thousands of staff persons in the executive and legislative branches, millions of work hours each year, and the active participation of the President and congressional leaders, as well as other Members of Congress and executive officials.

The enforcement of budgetary decisions involves a complex web of procedures that encompasses both congressional and executive actions. In the last three decades or so, these procedures have been rooted principally in two statutes—the Congressional Budget Act of 1974 and the Budget Enforcement Act (BEA). The 1974 act established a congressional budget process in which budget policies are enforced by Congress during the consideration of individual measures. The BEA is the most recent embodiment of additional enforcement procedures, first established in 1985 and renewed with substantial modification in 1990 and 1997, that have been used by the executive to enforce budget policies after the end of a congressional session. The BEA enforcement procedures were set aside in the latter years of their existence and effectively expired toward the end of the 107th Congress. Efforts to renew them in the 108th through 110th Congresses were not successful. In the 111th Congress, the pay-as-you-go procedures affecting direct spending and revenue legislation were restored in a modified version by the Statutory Pay-AsYou-Go Act of 2010.

The President's budget is required by law to be submitted to Congress early in the legislative session. While the budget is only a request to Congress, the power to formulate and submit the budget is a vital tool in the President's direction of the executive branch and of national policy. The President's proposals often influence congressional revenue and spending decisions, though the extent of the influence varies from year to year and depends more on political and fiscal conditions than on the legal status of the budget.

The Congressional Budget Act of 1974 establishes the congressional budget process as the means by which Congress coordinates the various budget-related actions (such as the consideration of appropriations and revenue measures) taken by it during the course of the year. The process is centered around an annual concurrent resolution on the budget that sets aggregate budget policies and functional spending priorities for at least the next five fiscal years. Because a concurrent resolution is not a law—it cannot be signed or vetoed by the President—the budget resolution does not have statutory effect; no money can be raised or spent pursuant to it. Revenue and spending amounts set in the budget resolution establish the basis for the enforcement of congressional budget policies through points of order.

Congress implements budget resolution policies through action on individual revenue and debt- limit measures, annual appropriations acts, and direct spending legislation. In some years, Congress considers reconciliation legislation pursuant to reconciliation instructions in the budget resolution. Reconciliation legislation is used mainly to bring existing revenue and direct spending laws into conformity with budget resolution policies Initially, reconciliation was a major tool for deficit reduction; in recent years, reconciliation has been used mainly to reduce revenues.

The Evolution of Federal Budgeting

The "power of the purse" is a legislative power. The Constitution lists the power to lay and collect taxes and the power to borrow as powers of Congress;

further, it provides that funds may be drawn from the Treasury only pursuant to appropriations made by law. The Constitution does not state how these legislative powers are to be exercised, nor does it expressly provide for the President to have a role in the management of the nation's finances.

During the nation's early years, the House and Senate devised procedures for the enactment of spending and revenue legislation. As these procedures evolved during the 19th century and the first decades of the 20th century, they led to highly fragmented legislative actions. In the course of each session, Congress passed many separate appropriations bills and other measures affecting the financial condition of the federal government. Neither the Constitution nor the procedures adopted by the House and Senate provided for a budget system—that is, for a coordinated set of actions covering all federal spending and revenues. As long as the federal government was small and its spending and revenues were stable, such a budget system was not considered necessary.

Early in the 20th century, the incessant rise in federal spending and the recurrence of deficits (spending exceeded revenues in half of the 20 years preceding FY1920) led Congress to seek a more coordinated means of making financial decisions. The key legislation was the Budget and Accounting Act of 1921, which established the executive budget process.

The 1921 act did not directly alter the procedures by which Congress makes revenue and spending decisions. The main impact was in the executive branch. The President was required to submit his budget recommendations to Congress each year, and the Bureau of the Budget— renamed the Office of Management and Budget (OMB) in 1 970—was created to assist him in carrying out his budgetary responsibilities. Congress, it was expected, would be able to coordinate its revenue and spending decisions if it received comprehensive budget recommendations from the President. In line with this expectation, the House and Senate changed their rules to consolidate the jurisdiction of the Appropriations Committees over spending. The 1921 act also established the General Accounting Office (GAO), headed by the Comptroller General, and made it the principal auditing arm of the federal government. (The GAO recently was renamed the Government Accountability Office.) The 1921 act, as amended, remains the statutory basis for the presidential budget system.

After World War II, the belief that the presidential budget sufficed to maintain fiscal control gave way to the view that Congress needed its own budget process. Some Members of Congress feared that dependence on the executive budget had bolstered the President's fiscal powers at the expense of

Congress's; others felt that as long as its financial decisions were fragmented, Congress could not effectively control expenditures.

The Congressional Budget and Impoundment Control Act of 1974 established a congressional budget process centered around a concurrent resolution on the budget, scheduled for adoption prior to legislative consideration of revenue or spending bills. The congressional budget process initiated in the 1970s did not replace the preexisting revenue and spending processes. Instead, it provided an overall legislative framework within which the many separate measures affecting the budget would be considered. The central purpose of the budget process established by the 1974 act is to coordinate the various revenue and spending decisions which are made in separate revenue, appropriations, and other budgetary measures. To assist Congress in making budget decisions, the 1974 act established the Congressional Budget Office (CBO) and directed it to provide data on and analyses of the federal budget.

During the years that the congressional budget process has been in operation, its procedures have been adapted by Congress to changing circumstances. Following a decade of experience with the 1974 Congressional Budget Act, Congress made further changes in the budget process by enacting the Balanced Budget and Emergency Deficit Control Act of 1985 (also known as the Gramm-Rudman-Hollings Act), the Budget Enforcement Act of 1990, the Line Item Veto Act in 1996, the Budget Enforcement Act of 1997, and the Statutory Pay-As-You-Go Act of 2010, among other laws.

The 1985 act prescribed declining deficit targets intended to achieve balance in FY1991; the targets were enforced by sequestration, a process involving automatic, across-the-board cuts in nonexempt spending programs if the targets were expected to be exceeded. The 1990 act replaced the deficit targets with caps on discretionary spending and a pay-as-you-go (PAYGO) requirement for revenue and direct spending legislation; sequestration was retained as the means of enforcing the two new mechanisms. The 1996 act authorized the President to cancel discretionary spending in appropriation acts, as well as new direct spending and limited tax benefits in other legislation, subject to expedited legislative procedures by which Congress could overturn the cancellations. (The Supreme Court struck down the Line Item Veto Act in June 1998 as unconstitutional.) The 1997 act extended the BEA procedures for several more years. Without a consensus on extending the control mechanisms under the BEA, however, they expired at the end of FY2002. The Statutory Pay-As-You-Go Act of 2010 restored a modified version of the PAYGO requirement for direct spending and revenue legislation. (The statutory caps on discretionary spending under the BEA have not been restored.)

BASIC CONCEPTS OF FEDERAL BUDGETING

The federal budget is a compilation of numbers about the revenues, spending, and borrowing and debt of the government. Revenues come largely from taxes, but stem from other sources as well (such as duties, fines, licenses, and gifts). Spending involves such concepts as budget authority, obligations, outlays, and offsetting collections. The numbers are computed according to rules and conventions that have accumulated over the years; they do not always conform to the way revenues and spending are accounted for in other processes.

Budget Authority and Outlays

When Congress appropriates money, it provides *budget authority*, that is, authority to enter into obligations. Budget authority also may be provided in legislation that does not go through the appropriations process (*direct spending* legislation). The key congressional spending decisions relate to the obligations that agencies are authorized to incur during a fiscal year, not to the outlays made during the year. (*Obligations* occur when agencies enter into contracts, submit purchase orders, employ personnel, and so forth; *outlays* occur when obligations are liquidated, primarily through the issuance of checks, electronic fund transfers, or the disbursement of cash.)

The provision of budget authority is the key point at which Congress exercises control over federal spending, although the outlay level often receives greater public attention because of its bearing on the deficit. Congress does not directly control outlays; each year's outlays derive in part from new budget authority and in part from "carryover" budget authority provided in prior years. For example, President Bush's initial budget submission for FY2009 estimated that outlays would total $3,107 billion for that year. Approximately $2,411 billion of this amount was estimated to come from new budget authority for the fiscal year, while the remainder ($696 billion) was estimated to come from budget authority enacted in prior years.

The relation of budget authority to outlays varies from program to program and depends on *spendout rates*, the rates at which funds provided by Congress are obligated and payments disbursed. In a program with a high spendout rate, most new budget authority is expended during the fiscal year; if the spendout rate is low, however, most of the outlays occur in later years. Regardless of the spendout rate, the outlays in the budget are merely estimates of the amounts that will be disbursed during the year. If payments turn out to be higher than the budget estimate, outlays will be above the budgeted level. The President and Congress control outlays indirectly by deciding on the amount of budget authority to be provided or by limiting the amount of obligations to be incurred.

Certain receipts of the federal government are accounted for as "offsets" against outlays rather than as revenues. Various fees collected by government agencies are deducted from outlays; similarly, income from the sale of certain assets are treated as *offsetting receipts*. Most such receipts are offsets against the outlays of the agencies that collect the money, but in the case of offshore oil leases and certain other activities, the revenues are deducted from the total outlays of the government.

Scope of the Budget

The budget consists of two main groups of funds: *federal funds* and *trust funds*. Federal funds— which comprise mainly the general fund—largely derive from the general exercise of the taxing power and general borrowing and for the most part are not earmarked by law to any specific program or agency. One component of federal funds, called special funds, are earmarked as to source and purpose. The use of federal funds is determined largely by appropriations acts.

Trust funds are established, under the terms of statutes that designate them as trust funds, to account for funds earmarked by specific sources and purposes. The Social Security funds are the largest of the trust funds; revenues are collected under a Social Security payroll tax and are used to pay for Social Security benefits and related purposes. The *unified budget* includes both the federal funds and the trust funds. The balances in the trust funds are borrowed by the federal government; they are counted, therefore, in the federal debt. Because these balances offset a budget deficit but are included in the federal debt, the annual increase in the debt invariably exceeds the amount of the budget deficit. For the same reason, it is possible for the federal debt to rise when the federal government has a budget surplus.

Capital and operating expenses are not segregated in the budget. Hence, monies paid for the operations of government agencies as well as for the acquisition of long-life assets (such as buildings, roads, and weapons systems) are reported as budget outlays. Proposals have been made from time to time to divide the budget into capital and operating accounts. While these proposals have not been adopted, the budget provides information showing the investment and operating outlays of the government.

The budget totals do not include all the financial transactions of the federal government. The main exclusions fall into two categories—off-budget entities and government-sponsored enterprises. In addition, the budget includes direct and guaranteed loans on the basis of the accounting rules established by the Federal Credit Reform Act of 1990, which are discussed below.

Off-budget entities are excluded by law from the budget totals. The receipts and disbursements of the Social Security trust funds (the Old-Age and Survivors Insurance Fund and the Disability Insurance Fund), as well as spending for the Postal Service Fund, are excluded from the budget totals. These transactions are shown separately in the budget. Thus, the budget now reports two deficit or surplus amounts—one excluding the Social Security trust funds and the Postal Service Fund, and the other (on a unified basis) including these entities. The latter is the main focus of discussion in both the President's budget and the congressional budget process.

The transactions of government-owned corporations (excluding the Postal Service), as well as revolving funds, are included in the budget on a net basis. That is, the amount shown in the budget is the difference between receipts and outlays, not the total activity of the enterprise or revolving fund. If, for example, a revolving fund has annual income of $150 million and disbursements of $200 million, the budget would report $50 million as net outlays.

Government-sponsored enterprises (GSEs) historically have been excluded from the budget because they were deemed to be private rather than public entities. The federal government did not own any equity in these enterprises, most of which received their financing from private sources. Although they were established by the federal government, their budgets were not reviewed by the President or Congress in the same manner as other programs. Most of these enterprises engaged in credit activities. They borrowed funds in capital markets and lent money to homeowners, farmers, and others. In total, these enterprises had assets and liabilities measured in trillions of dollars. Financial statements of the government-sponsored enterprises were published in the President's budget.

Although some GSEs continue to operate on this basis, the economic downturn and credit instability that occurred in 2008 fundamentally changed the status of two GSEs that play a significant role in the home mortgage market, Fannie Mae and Freddie Mac. In September of 2008, the Federal Housing Finance Agency (FHFA) placed the two entities in conservatorship, thereby subjecting them to control by the Federal Government until the conservatorship eventually is brought to an end.

Deficit Reduction and the Rules of Congressional Budgeting

Between the early 1980s and the late 1990s, annual consideration of the budget was dominated by concern about the budget deficit. In the mid-1980s, the deficit exceeded $150 billion and amounted to about 6% of GDP at one point. In the early 1990s, the deficit approached the $300 billion level. Following four years of surpluses (FY1998-FY2001), the budget returned to deficit for FY2002. Current budget projections show sizeable deficits persisting over the coming years.

The size of the deficit depends on how it is measured. The unified budget deficit combines all on- budget federal funds and trust funds with the off-budget entities (the Social Security trust funds and the Postal Service Fund). The unified budget deficit generally is regarded as the most comprehensive measure of the impact of the budget on the economy. A narrower measure of the deficit is derived by excluding the Social Security trust funds from the totals. This exclusion is mandated by law, although Social Security is counted in the budget in reports on the deficit. Excluding Social Security from computations of the deficit or surplus results in higher deficit or lower surplus figures.

Regardless of the measure used, it is evident that the deficit was unusually high for an extended period of time. The chronic deficits of the 1980s prompted Congress to enact the Balanced Budget and Emergency Deficit Control Act of 1985. The 1985 act established deficit targets for each year through FY1991, when the budget was to be balanced, and a sequestration process under which budgetary resources would be canceled automatically (through largely across-the- board spending cuts) if the estimated deficit exceeded the amount allowed under the act.

Even with the targets, the actual deficit for the covered years was above the targeted level. Failure to achieve the deficit targets, and other problems, led Congress to revise the process in the Budget Enforcement Act (BEA) of 1990. Sequestration procedures were retained, but the fixed deficit targets were replaced by adjustable ones (which expired at the end of FY1995), adjustable limits were imposed on discretionary spending, and a pay-as-you-go (PAYGO) process was established for revenues and direct spending. The discretionary spending limits and PAYGO process were extended (through FY1998) by the Omnibus Budget Reconciliation of 1993 and again (through FY2002) by the BEA of 1997.

Under the discretionary spending limits, different categories of discretionary spending were used for different periods. Under the 1997 changes, discretionary spending limits applied separately to defense and nondefense spending for FY1998-FY1999 and to violent crime reduction spending for FY1998-FY2000; for the remaining fiscal years, the 1997 changes merged all discretionary spending into a single, general purpose category. In 1998, as part of the Transportation Equity Act for the 21st Century, Congress added separate categories for highway and mass transit spending. Finally, in 2000, Congress added a category for conservation spending; unlike the other categories, the conservation spending category had six subcategories.

The PAYGO process under the BEA required that the budgetary impact of revenue and direct spending legislation be recorded on a multiyear "PAYGO scorecard," and that in the net any such legislation not yield a negative balance for the upcoming fiscal year. Legislation reducing revenues or increasing direct spending for a fiscal year had to be offset (in the same or other legislation) by revenue increases or reductions in direct spending for that fiscal year so that the applicable balance on the PAYGO scorecard remained at or above zero.

Under the BEA procedures, violations of the discretionary spending limits or the PAYGO requirement were to be enforced by sequestration. However, sequestration was not used for more than a decade, either because Congress and the President enacted budgetary legislation consistent with the discretionary spending limits and PAYGO requirement, or, during the latter years under the BEA, effectively waived these enforcement requirements.

The BEA enforcement procedures effectively expired toward the end of the 107th Congress. As budget deficits persisted through the last decade, proposals to restore the BEA statutory procedures had been made from time to time by Members of Congress and the President, but none of the proposals were enacted until 2010. The Statutory Pay-As-You-Go Act of 2010 (P.L. 111-139) restored in statute a modified version of the PAYGO requirement for direct spending and revenue legislation.[1] The statutory caps on discretionary spending under the BEA, however, have not been restored.

Like the previous statutory PAYGO requirement under the BEA, the new statutory PAYGO requirement is intended to discourage or prevent Congress from taking certain legislative action that would increase the on-budget deficit. It generally requires that legislation affecting direct spending or revenues not increase the deficit over a six-year period and an 11-year period.

The PAYGO statute exempts certain direct spending and revenue provisions from being counted for purposes of the PAYGO requirement: (1) provisions designated as an emergency; and (2) provisions extending current policy in four specified areas, which are scheduled by statute to expire, within certain constraints. The four current policy areas include (1) Medicare payments to physicians, (2) estate and gift tax, (3) alternative minimum tax (AMT), and (4) middle-class tax cuts.

The statutory PAYGO requirement is enforced by sequestration—the cancellation of budgetary resources provided by laws affecting direct spending—to eliminate an increase in the deficit resulting from the enactment of legislation. Generally, the statutory PAYGO rule provides that if the net effect of direct spending and revenue legislation enacted during a year increases the deficit (i.e., violates the PAYGO requirement), budgetary resources in certain direct spending programs are cut in order to eliminate the increase in the deficit.

Most direct spending programs and activities, including Social Security benefits, veterans' programs, retirement and disability benefits, and low-income programs, among others, are exempt from any sequestration. In addition, the amount of any sequestration is limited to 4% for Medicare and 2% for certain health and medical care activities.

During the 1990s to the present, the Senate has supplemented the statutory PAYGO requirement with a special PAYGO rule included in annual budget resolutions; following the expiration of the BEA procedures, the Senate extended its PAYGO rule (currently through FY20 17). The House adopted its own PAYGO rule for the first time at the beginning of the 110th Congress. Although the Senate PAYGO rule has been revised significantly from time to time, it presently is similar in approach to the House rule. Both rules provide for points of order to bar the consideration of any legislation that proposes changes in direct spending or revenue that are not deficit neutral over six-year and 11-year time periods (including the current fiscal year).

BUDGETING FOR DISCRETIONARY AND DIRECT SPENDING

The distinction drawn by the BEA and the congressional budget process between discretionary spending (which is controlled through the annual appropriations process) and direct spending (which is provided outside of the annual appropriations process) recognized that the federal government has somewhat different, though overlapping, means of dealing with these two types of spending. One set of procedures pertained to discretionary spending, another to direct spending.

Most of the direct spending subject to the PAYGO process under the BEA involved entitlement programs; the rest consisted of other forms of mandatory spending provided through authorizing legislation and interest payments. In fact, entitlements now account for about half of total federal spending (all direct spending, including net interest, accounts for about 60% of the total). The impressive feature of this trend is that most of the growth in spending and in the number of recipients has been built into existing law; for the most part, it has not been the result of new legislation.

The procedures for discretionary and direct spending converge at two critical points in federal budgeting: formulation of the President's budget and formulation of the congressional budget resolution. Both of these policy statements encompass discretionary and direct spending, but the procedures used in budgeting for these types of expenditure differ greatly. The distinctions have some notable exceptions. Some procedures associated with direct spending are applied to particular types of discretionary programs, and vice versa. Nevertheless, the generalizations presented here help to explain the complications of the budget process and explain how decisions are made.

(1) *Budgetary Impact of Authorizing Legislation.* An authorization for a discretionary spending program is only a license to enact an appropriation. The amount of budgetary resources available for spending is determined in annual appropriations acts. For direct spending programs (principally entitlements), on the other hand, the authorizing legislation either provides, or effectively mandates the appropriation of, budget authority. In those entitlement programs that

are subject to annual appropriation, the Appropriations Committees have little or no discretion as to the amounts they provide.

(2) *Committees That Provide or Mandate Budget Authority.* The Appropriations Committees have jurisdiction and effective control over discretionary spending programs, while authorizing committees effectively control direct spending programs (including those funded in annual appropriations acts). In fact, committee jurisdiction determines whether a program is classified as discretionary or direct spending. All spending under the effective control of the Appropriations Committees is discretionary; everything else is direct spending. Accordingly, when legislation establishes a program as discretionary or direct spending, it not only determines the character of spending but the locus of congressional committee control as well.

(3) *Frequency of Decision-Making.* Discretionary appropriations are, with few exceptions, made annually for the current or next fiscal year. Direct spending programs typically are established in permanent law that continues in effect until such time as it is revised or terminated by another law. The fact that many entitlements have annual appropriations does not diminish the permanence of the laws governing the amounts spent. It should be noted, however, that some direct spending programs, such as Medicare, have been subject to frequent legislative changes. The purpose of such legislation has been to modify existing law, not to provide annual funding.

(4) *Means of Enforcing the Budget Resolution.* The procedures used by Congress to enforce the policies set forth in the annual budget resolution differ somewhat for discretionary and direct spending programs. For both types of spending, Congress relies on allocations made under Section 302 of the 1974 Congressional Budget Act to ensure that spending legislation reported by House and Senate committees conforms to established budget policies. But although this procedure is effective in controlling new legislation—both annual appropriations measures and new entitlement legislation—it is not an effective control on the spending that results from existing laws. Hence, Congress relies on reconciliation procedures to enforce budget policies with respect to existing spending and revenue laws. Reconciliation is not currently applied to discretionary programs funded in annual appropriations measures.

(5) *Statutory Controls.* Discretionary programs have been subject to the spending limits set in the BEA. Direct spending has not been capped,

> but has operated under the PAYGO process, which required that direct spending and revenue legislation enacted for a fiscal year not cause the deficit to rise or the surplus to decrease. The lack of caps was due to the fact that most direct spending programs are open-ended, with spending determined by eligibility rules and payment formulas in existing law rather than by new legislation.

Budget enforcement depends on timely information concerning the status of federal revenues and spending. When it acts on legislation, Congress must be informed of the estimated impact on future budgets. Measuring these impacts often is referred to as “scoring” or “scorekeeping.” Scoring discretionary spending measures is a much simpler task than scoring direct spending and revenue legislation. In the latter case, scoring always is done in reference to baseline projections of future revenues and spending.

Most appropriations are for a definite amount and the budget authority is provided for a single fiscal year. The main task is to estimate the outlays that will derive in the next year and beyond from the budget authority provided in the appropriations bill. CBO and the Appropriations Committees base these estimates on outlay (or spendout) rates—the percentage of budget authority that is spent in each year. These outlay rates vary by account and are based on historical records. For example, if $1 billion is appropriated to an account which has a spendout rate of 80% in the first fiscal year that funds become available, the outlay estimate for that fiscal year will be $800 million; the remaining $200 million will become outlays in one or more subsequent years.

Scorekeeping is much more complex in enforcing a PAYGO requirement. For one thing, unlike appropriations, revenue and direct spending legislation usually is open-ended; it does not specify the amount by which revenue or spending will be changed. For another, the impact of this type of legislation continues in future years. In enforcing the PAYGO requirements, Congress had to estimate the revenue gain or loss for the ensuing five years under the BEA, and for 11 years under the more recent statutory and congressional PAYGO rules. Congress cannot develop the revenue estimates simply by referring to the text of the legislation being scored. It must also take into account the behavior of taxpayers, economic conditions, and other factors that affect revenue collection.

Congress scores revenue and direct spending legislation by reference to baseline projections issued by CBO, sometimes in cooperation with OMB. The baseline is an extrapolation of future budget conditions, typically for each of the next five years, based on the assumption that current policies will continue in effect. The baseline projections incorporate assumptions about future inflation and workload changes mandated by law. These projections are made for the budget aggregates as well as for individual programs and accounts.

When Congress considers revenue or direct spending legislation, CBO estimates the amount of revenues or outlays that would ensue if the measure were enacted; in the case of most revenue legislation, CBO uses estimates prepared by the Joint Tax Committee. It then compares this amount with the baseline projection to score the legislation. Thus, the score measures budgetary impact as the difference between the amount projected under current policies and the amount estimated if the legislation were enacted. A score is reported for each of the years and often for the sum of the years as well.

Congress usually relies on the CBO score while it is considering legislation. The BEA gave OMB the authority to determine whether offsets or a sequester were required under the PAYGO rules. The recent Statutory Pay-As-You-Go Act of 2010 provides that the budgetary effects of individual direct spending and revenue legislation are to be determined either by a reference in the legislation to a statement of budgetary effects submitted for printing in the *Congressional Record* by the chair of the House or Senate Budget Committee prior to passage, or by OMB if no appropriate reference in the legislation or statement exists. The OMB and CBO scores on legislation sometimes differ.

In addition to enforcing PAYGO, baseline projections and scoring are used in computing the amount of deficit reduction agreed to in budget summit negotiations between the President and Congress and enacted in reconciliation acts.

BUDGETING FOR DIRECT AND GUARANTEED LOANS

The Federal Credit Reform Act of 1990 made fundamental changes in the budgetary treatment of direct loans and guaranteed loans. The reform, which first became effective for FY1992, shifted the accounting basis for federally provided or guaranteed credit from the amount of cash flowing into or out of the Treasury to the estimated subsidy cost of the loans. Credit reform entails complex procedures for estimating these subsidy costs and new accounting mechanisms for recording various loan transactions. The changes have had only a modest impact on budget totals but a substantial impact on budgeting for particular loan programs.

The new system requires that budget authority and outlays be budgeted for the estimated subsidy cost of direct and guaranteed loans. This cost is defined in the 1990 act as "the estimated longterm cost to the Government of a direct loan or a loan guarantee, calculated on a net present value basis, excluding administrative costs...."

Under the new system, Congress appropriates budget authority or provides indefinite authority equal to the subsidy cost. This budget authority is placed in a program account from which funds are disbursed to a financing account.

THE BUDGET CYCLE

Federal budgeting is a cyclical activity that begins with the formulation of the President's annual budget and concludes with the audit and review of expenditures. The process spreads over a multi-year period. The main stages are formulation of the President's budget, congressional budget actions, implementation of the budget, and audit and review. While the basic steps continue from year to year, particular procedures often vary in accord with the style of the President, the economic and political considerations under which the budget is prepared and implemented, and other factors.

The activities related to a single fiscal year usually stretch over a period of two-and-a-half calendar years (or longer). As the budget is being considered, federal agencies must deal with three different fiscal years at the same time: implementing the budget for the current fiscal year; seeking funds from Congress for the next fiscal year; and planning for the fiscal year after that.

THE PRESIDENTIAL BUDGET PROCESS

The President's budget, officially referred to as the *Budget of the United States Government*, is required by law to be submitted to Congress early in the legislative session, no later than the first Monday in February. The budget consists of estimates of spending, revenues, borrowing, and debt; policy and legislative recommendations; detailed estimates of the financial operations of federal agencies and programs; data on the actual and projected performance of the economy; and other information supporting the President's recommendations.

The President's budget is only a request to Congress; Congress is not required to adopt his recommendations. Nevertheless, the power to formulate and submit the budget is a vital tool in the President's direction of the executive branch and of national policy. The President's proposals often influence congressional revenue and spending decisions, though the extent of the influence varies from year to year and depends more on political and fiscal conditions than on the legal status of the budget.

The Constitution does not provide for a budget, nor does it require the President to make recommendations concerning the revenues and spending of the federal government. Until 1921, the federal government operated without a comprehensive presidential budget process. The Budget and Accounting Act of 1921, as amended, provides for a national budget system. Its basic requirement is that the President should prepare and submit a budget to Congress each year. The 1921 act established the Bureau of the Budget, now named the Office of Management and Budget (OMB), to assist the President in preparing and implementing the executive budget. Although it has been amended many times, this statute provides the legal basis for the presidential budget, prescribes much of its content, and defines the roles of the President and the agencies in the process.

Formulation and Content of the President's Budget

Preparation of the President's budget typically begins in the spring (or earlier) each year, at least nine months before the budget is submitted to Congress, about 17 months before the start of the fiscal year to which it pertains, and about 29 months before the close of that fiscal year. The early stages of budget preparation occur in federal agencies. When they begin work on the budget for a fiscal year, agencies already are implementing the budget for the fiscal year in progress and awaiting final appropriations actions and other legislative decisions for the fiscal year after that. The long lead times and the fact that appropriations have not yet been made for the next year mean that the budget is prepared with a great deal of uncertainty about economic conditions, presidential policies, and congressional actions.

As agencies formulate their budgets, they maintain continuing contact with the OMB examiners assigned to them. These contacts provide agencies with guidance in preparing their budgets and also enable them to alert OMB to any needs or problems that may loom ahead. Agency requests are submitted to OMB in late summer or early fall; these are reviewed by OMB staff in consultation with the President and his aides. The 1921 Budget and Accounting Act bars agencies from submitting their budget requests directly to Congress. Moreover, OMB regulations provide for confidentiality in all budget requests and recommendations prior to the transmittal of the President's budget to Congress. However, it is quite common for internal budget documents to become public while the budget is still being formulated.

The format and content of the budget are partly determined by law, but the 1921 act authorizes the President to set forth the budget "in such form and detail" as he may determine. Over the years, there has been an increase in the types of information and explanatory material presented in the budget documents.

In most years, the budget is submitted as a multi-volume set consisting of a main document setting forth the President's message to Congress and an analysis and justification of his major proposals (the *Budget*) and supplementary documents providing account and program level details, historical information, and special budgetary analyses (the *Budget Appendix*, *Historical Tables*, and *Analytical Perspectives*), among other things.

Much of the budget is an estimate of requirements under existing law rather than a request for congressional action (more than half of the budget authority in the budget becomes available without congressional action). The President is required to submit a budget update (reflecting changed economic conditions, congressional actions, and other factors), referred to as the *Mid-Session Review*, by July 15 each year. The President may revise his recommendations any time during the year.

Executive Interaction with Congress

The President and his budget office have an important role once the budget is submitted to Congress. OMB officials and other presidential advisors appear before congressional committees to discuss overall policy and economic issues, but they generally leave formal discussions of specific programs to the affected agencies. Agencies thus bear the principal responsibility for defending the President's program recommendations at congressional hearings.

Agencies are supposed to justify the President's recommendations, not their own. OMB maintains an elaborate legislative clearance process to ensure that agency budget justifications, testimony, and other submissions are consistent with presidential policy. As the session unfolds, the President may formally signal his position on pending legislation through the issuance of a Statement of Administration Policy (SAP). These statements, which are maintained by OMB on its website, sometimes are used to convey a veto threat against legislation the President feels requires modifications to meet his approval.

Increasingly in recent years, the President and his chief budgetary aides have engaged in extensive negotiations with Congress over major budgetary legislation. These negotiations sometimes have occurred as formal budget "summits" and at other times as less visible, behindthe-scenes activities.

THE CONGRESSIONAL BUDGET PROCESS

The Congressional Budget and Impoundment Control Act of 1974 establishes the congressional budget process as the means by which Congress coordinates the various budget-related actions (such as the consideration of appropriations and revenue measures) taken by it during the course of the year. The process is centered around an annual concurrent resolution on the budget that sets aggregate budget policies and functional priorities for at least the next five fiscal years.

Because a concurrent resolution is not a law—it cannot be signed or vetoed by the President—the budget resolution does not have statutory effect; no money can be raised or spent pursuant to it. The main purpose of the budget resolution is to establish the framework within which Congress considers separate revenue, spending, and other budget-related legislation. Revenue and spending amounts set in the budget resolution establish the basis for the enforcement of congressional budget policies through points of order. The budget resolution also initiates the reconciliation process for conforming existing revenue and spending laws to congressional budget policies.

Formulation and Content of the Budget Resolution

The congressional budget process begins upon the presentation of the President's budget in January or February (see **Table 1**). The timetable set forth in the 1974 Congressional Budget Act calls for the final adoption of the budget resolution by April 15, well before the beginning of the new fiscal year on October 1. Although the House and Senate often pass the budget resolution separately before April 15, they often do not reach final agreement on it until after the deadline— sometimes months later. The 1974 act bars consideration of revenue, spending, and debt-limit measures for the upcoming fiscal year until the budget resolution for that year has been adopted, but certain exceptions are provided (such as the exception that allows the House to consider the regular appropriations bills after May 15, even if the budget resolution has not been adopted by then).

The 1974 Congressional Budget Act requires the budget resolution, for each fiscal year covered, to set forth budget aggregates and spending levels for each functional category of the budget. The aggregates included in the budget resolution are as follows:

Table 1. Congressional Budget Process Timetable

Deadline	Action to be completed
First Monday in February	President submits budget to Congress.
February 15	CBO submits report on economic and budget outlook to Budget committees.
Six weeks after President's budget is submitted	Committees submit reports on views and estimates to respective Budget Committee.
April 1	Senate Budget Committee reports budget resolution.
April 15	Congress completes action on budget resolution.
June 10	House Appropriations Committee reports last regular appropriations bill.
June 30	House completes action on regular appropriations bills and any required reconciliation legislation.
July 15	President submits mid-session review of his budget to Congress.
October 1	Fiscal year begins.

Source: Compiled by the Congressional Research Service.

- total revenues (and the amount by which the total is to be changed by legislative action);
- total new budget authority and outlays;
- the surplus or deficit; and
- the debt limit.

With regard to each of the functional categories, the budget resolution must indicate for each fiscal year the amounts of new budget authority and outlays, and they must add up to the corresponding spending or aggregates.

Aggregate amounts in the budget resolution do not reflect the revenues or spending of the Social Security trust funds, although these amounts are set forth separately in the budget resolution for purposes of Senate enforcement procedures.

The budget resolution does not allocate funds among specific programs or accounts, but the major program assumptions underlying the functional amounts are often discussed in the reports accompanying each resolution. Some recent reports have contained detailed information on the program levels assumed in the resolution. These assumptions are not binding on the affected committees. Finally, the 1974 act allows certain additional matters to be included in the budget resolution. The most important optional feature of a budget resolution is reconciliation directives (discussed below).

The House and Senate Budget Committees are responsible for marking up and reporting the budget resolution. In the course of developing the budget resolution, the Budget Committees hold hearings, receive "views and estimates" reports from other committees, and obtain information from CBO. These "views and estimates" reports of House and Senate committees provide the Budget Committees with information on the preferences and legislative plans of congressional committees regarding budgetary matters within their jurisdiction.

CBO assists the Budget Committees in developing the budget resolution by issuing, early each year, a report on the economic and budget outlook that includes baseline budget projections. The baseline projections presented in the report are supported by more detailed projections for accounts and programs; CBO usually revises the baseline projections one or more times before the Budget Committees mark up the budget resolution. In addition, CBO issues a report analyzing the President's budgetary proposals in light of CBO's own economic and technical assumptions. In past years, CBO also issued an annual report on spending and revenue options for reducing the deficit or maintaining the surplus.

The extent to which the Budget Committees (and the House and Senate) consider particular programs when they act on the budget resolution varies from year to year. Specific program decisions are supposed to be left to the Appropriations Committees and other committees of jurisdiction, but there is a strong likelihood that major issues will be discussed in markup, in the Budget Committees' reports, and during floor consideration of the budget resolution.

Although any programmatic assumptions generated in this process are not binding on the committees of jurisdiction, they often influence the final outcome.

Floor consideration of the budget resolution is guided by House and Senate rules and practices. In the House, the Rules Committee usually reports a *special rule* (a simple House resolution), which, once approved, establishes the terms and conditions under which the budget resolution is considered. This special rule typically specifies which amendments may be considered and the sequence in which they are to be offered and voted on. It has been the practice in recent years to allow consideration of a few amendments (as substitutes for the entire resolution) that present broad policy choices. In the Senate, the amendment process is less structured, relying on agreements reached by the leadership through a broad consultative process. The amendments offered in the Senate may entail major policy choices or may be focused on a single issue.

Achievement of the policies set forth in the annual budget resolution depends on the legislative actions taken by Congress (and their approval or disapproval by the President), the performance of the economy, and technical considerations. Many of the factors that determine whether budgetary goals will be met are beyond the direct control of Congress. If economic conditions— growth, employment levels, inflation, and so forth—vary significantly from projected levels, so too will actual levels of revenue and spending. Similarly, actual levels may differ substantially if the technical factors upon which estimates are based, such as the rate at which agencies spend their discretionary funds or participants become eligible for entitlement programs, prove faulty.

Budget Resolution Enforcement

Congress's regular tools for enforcing the budget resolution each year are overall spending ceilings and revenue floors and committee allocations and subdivisions of spending. In addition, the Senate in some years has enforced discretionary spending limits in the budget resolution, which paralleled the adjustable limits established in statute and enforced by the sequestration process, and both chambers have imposed PAYGO rules on direct spending and revenue legislation. Finally, the House and Senate in recent years have included procedural features in budget resolutions to limit the use of advance appropriations.

In order for the enforcement procedures to work, Congress must have access to complete and up- to-date budgetary information so that it can relate individual measures to overall budget policies and determine whether adoption of a particular measure would be consistent with those policies. Substantive and procedural points of order are designed to obtain congressional compliance with budget rules. A point of order may bar House or Senate consideration of legislation that violates the spending ceilings and revenue floors in the budget resolution, committee subdivisions of spending, or congressional budget procedures.

Budget Resolution Aggregates

In the early years after the 1974 Congressional Budget Act, the principal enforcement mechanism was the ceiling on total budget authority and outlays and the floor under total revenues set forth in the budget resolution. The limitations inherent in this mechanism soon became apparent. For example, the issue of controlling breaches of the spending ceilings usually did not arise until Congress acted on supplemental appropriations acts, when the fiscal year was well underway. The emergency nature of the legislation often made it difficult to uphold the ceilings.

Changes sometimes are made in budget resolutions by virtue of the operation of reserve funds. Generally, reserve funds allow increases to be made in various spending levels associated with the budget resolution for legislation meeting criteria specified in the budget resolution, as long as any increases spending from the legislation is offset (e.g., by revenue increases) so as to be deficit neutral.

Allocations of Spending to Committees

In view of the inadequacies in the early years of congressional budgeting of relying on enforcement of the budget totals, Congress changed the focus of enforcement in the 1980s to the committee allocations and subdivisions of spending made pursuant to Section 302 of the act. The key to enforcing budget policy is to relate the budgetary impact of individual pieces of legislation to the overall budget policy. Because Congress operates through its committee system, an essential step in linking particular measures to the budget is to allocate the spending amounts set forth in the budget resolution among House and Senate committees.

Section 302(a) provides for allocations to committees to be made in the statement of managers accompanying the conference report on the budget resolution. A Section 302(a) allocation is made to each committee which has jurisdiction over spending, both for the budget year and the full period covered by the budget resolution—at least five fiscal years.

The committee allocations do not take into account jurisdiction over discretionary authorizations funded in annual appropriations acts. The amounts of new budget authority and outlays allocated to committees in the House or Senate may not exceed the aggregate amounts of budget authority and outlays set forth in the budget resolution. Although these allocations are made by the Budget Committees, they are not the unilateral preferences of these committees. They are based on assumptions and understandings developed in the course of formulating the budget resolution.

After the allocations are made under Section 302(a), the House and Senate Appropriations Committees subdivide the amounts they receive among their 12 subcommittees, as required by Section 302(b). The subcommittees' Section 302(b) subdivisions may not exceed the total amount allocated to the committee. Each Appropriations Committee reports its subdivisions to its respective chamber; the appropriations bills may not be considered until such a report has been filed.

Scoring and Cost Estimates

As mentioned previously, scoring (also called scorekeeping) is the process of measuring the budgetary effects of pending and enacted legislation and assessing its impact on a budget plan— in this case, the budget resolution. In the congressional budget process, scoring serves several broad purposes. First, scoring informs Members of Congress and the public about the budgetary consequences of their actions. When a budgetary measure is under consideration, scoring information lets Members know whether adopting the amendment or passing the bill at hand would breach the budget. Further, scoring information enables Members to judge what must be done in upcoming legislative action to achieve the year's budgetary goals. Finally, scoring is designed to assist Congress in enforcing its budget plans. In this regard, scorekeeping is used largely to determine whether points of order under the 1974 act may be sustained against legislation violating budget resolution levels.

The principal scorekeepers for Congress are the House and Senate Budget Committees, which provide the presiding officers of their respective chambers with the estimates needed to determine if legislation violates the aggregate levels in the budget resolution or the committee subdivisions of spending. The Budget Committees make summary scoring reports available to Members on a frequent basis, usually geared to the pace of legislative activity. CBO assists

Congress in these activities by preparing cost estimates of legislation, which are included in committee reports, and scoring reports for the Budget committees. The Joint Committee on Taxation supports Congress by preparing estimates of the budgetary impact of revenue legislation.

Points of Order

The 1974 Congressional Budget Act provides for both substantive and procedural points of order to block violations of budget resolution policies and congressional budget procedures. One element of substantive enforcement is based on Section 311 of the act, which bars Congress from considering legislation that would cause total revenues to fall below the level set in the budget resolution or total new budget authority or total outlays to exceed the budgeted level. The House and Senate both enforce the spending ceilings for the first fiscal year only; the revenue floor, however, is enforced for the first fiscal year and the full number of fiscal years covered by the budget resolution.

In the House (but not the Senate), Section 311 does not apply to spending legislation if the committee reporting the measure has stayed within its allocation of new discretionary budget authority. Accordingly, the House may take up any spending measure that is within the appropriate committee allocations, even if it would cause total spending to be exceeded. Neither chamber bars spending legislation that would cause functional allocations in the budget resolution to be exceeded.

Section 302(f) of the 1974 act bars the House and Senate from considering any spending measure that would cause the relevant committee's spending allocations to be exceeded; in the House, the point of order applies only to violations of allocations of new discretionary budget authority. Further, the point of order also applies to suballocations of spending made by the Appropriations Committees.

In addition to points of order to enforce compliance with the budget resolution and the allocations and subdivisions made pursuant to it, the 1974 act contains points of order to ensure compliance with its procedures. Perhaps the most important of these is Section 303, which bars consideration of any revenue, spending, entitlement, or debt-limit measure prior to adoption of the budget resolution. However, the rules of the House permit it to consider regular appropriations bills after May 15, even if the budget resolution has not yet been adopted.

When the House or Senate considers a revenue or a spending measure, the chairman of the respective Budget Committee sometimes makes a statement advising the chamber as to whether the measure violates any of these points of order. If no point of order is made, or if the point of order is waived, the House or Senate may consider a measure despite any violations of the 1974 act. The House often waives points of order by adopting a special rule. The Senate may waive points of order by unanimous consent or by motion under Section 904 of the act. The Senate requires a three-fifths vote of the membership to waive certain provisions of the act.

In five instances, in 1998 (for FY1999), 2002 (for FY2003), 2004 (for FY2005), 2006 (for FY2007), and 2010 (for FY2011), the House and Senate failed to reach agreement on a budget resolution. On these occasions, one or both houses agreed to their own "deeming resolutions," which established the basis for enforcing points of order under the 1974 act in that house only.

THE SEQUESTRATION PROCESS

Sequestration was the principle means used to enforce statutory budget enforcement policies in place from 1985 through 2002, and it is the principle means used to enforce the more recently enacted PAYGO requirement under the Statutory Pay-As-You-Go Act of 2010.

Sequestration involves the issuance of a presidential order that permanently cancelled budgetary resources (except for revolving funds, special funds, trust funds, and certain offsetting collections) for the purpose of achieving a required amount of outlay savings to reduce the deficit. Once sequestration is triggered by an executive determination, spending reductions are made automatically; this process, therefore, is regarded by many as providing a strong incentive for Congress and the President to reach agreement on legislation that would avoid a sequester.

From its inception in 1985 until its revision by the Budget Enforcement Act (BEA) in 1990, the process was tied solely to the enforcement of fixed deficit targets. The BEA changed the sequestration process substantially. First, it effectively eliminated the deficit targets as a factor in budget enforcement. Second, the BEA established adjustable limits on discretionary spending funded in the annual appropriations process. Third, the BEA created pay-as-you-go procedures to require that increases in direct spending (i.e., spending controlled outside of the annual appropriations process) or decreases in revenues due to legislative action were offset so that there was effectively no net increase in the deficit or reduction of the surplus.

The BEA established adjustable limits on discretionary spending for FY1 991 -FY1 995. These limits were extended through FY1998 in 1993. The Budget Enforcement Act (BEA) of 1997 revised the limits for FY1998 and provided new limits through FY2002. The limits were established for the following categories of discretionary spending: defense and nondefense, for FY1998-FY1999; discretionary (a single, general purpose category), for FY2000-FY2002; and violent crime reduction, for FY1 998-FY2000. In 1998, as part of the Transportation Equity Act for the 21st Century, separate categories were added for highway and mass transit spending. Finally, a spending conservation category was added in 2000. The limits expired at the end of FY2002. Since then, interest in renewing them has arisen periodically. It is unclear at this point whether Congress will decide to revive them.

The discretionary spending limits had to be adjusted periodically by the President for various factors, including (among others), changes in concepts and definitions, a special outlay allowance (to accommodate estimating differences between OMB and CBO), and the enactment of legislation providing emergency funding and funding for the International Monetary Fund, international arrearages, an earned income tax credit compliance initiative, and other specially- designated purposes.

Under the pay-as-you-go (PAYGO) process created by the BEA, legislation increasing direct spending or decreasing revenues for a fiscal year had to be offset so that the balance on the PAYGO scorecard for that year did not fall below zero. The PAYGO process did not require any offsetting action when the spending increase or revenue decrease was due to the operation of existing law, such as an increase in the number of persons participating in the Medicare program. Direct spending consists largely of spending for entitlement programs. Most direct spending and revenue programs are established under permanent law, so there is not necessarily any need for recurring legislative action on them (and the PAYGO process did not require such action).

The PAYGO process did not preclude Congress from enacting legislation to increase direct spending; it only required that the increase be offset by reductions in other direct spending programs (which could include increases in offsetting receipts), by increases in revenues, or by a combination of the two in order to avoid a sequester. If a sequester under this process was required, it would have had to offset the amount of any net deficit increase (or surplus reduction) for the fiscal year caused by the enactment of legislation in the current and prior sessions of Congress, and would have been applied to nonexempt direct spending programs.

Spending for Social Security benefits and federal deposit insurance commitments, as well as emergency direct spending and revenue legislation (so designated by both the President and by Congress), was exempted completely from the PAYGO sequestration process. All remaining direct spending programs were covered by the PAYGO process to the extent that legislation affecting their spending levels was counted in determining whether a net increase or decrease in the deficit has occurred for a fiscal year. If a PAYGO sequester had occurred, however, many direct spending programs would have been exempt from reduction.

In 1997, coverage of the PAYGO requirement was extended to legislation enacted through FY2002; however, the PAYGO process was slated to remain in effect through FY2006 to deal with the outyear effects of such measures. Consequently, a PAYGO sequester could have occurred in FY2003-FY2006 based on legislation enacted before the end of FY2002. At the end of the 107th Congress, legislation was enacted setting all of the remaining PAYGO balances to zero, effectively terminating the PAYGO requirement under the BEA.

The multiple sequestration procedures established by the BEA remained automatic, to be triggered by a report from the OMB director. For sequestration purposes generally, there was only one triggering report issued each year (just after the end of the congressional session), but preliminary and update sequestration reports were issued earlier in the session. Additionally, OMB reports triggering a sequester for discretionary spending could be issued during the following session if legislative developments so warranted (i.e., the enactment of supplemental appropriations). The CBO director was required to provide advisory sequestration reports, shortly before the OMB director's reports were due.

Sequestration procedures could be suspended in the event a declaration of war was enacted or if Congress enacted a special joint resolution triggered by the issuance of a CBO report indicating "low growth" in the economy. Also, there were several special procedures under the act by which the final sequestration order for a fiscal year could be modified or the implementation of the order affected.

As noted above, the BEA procedures, including the accompanying sequestration process, effectively expired toward the end of the 107th Congress. The Statutory Pay-As-You-Go Act of 2010, enacted on February 12, 2010, restored the sequestration process to enforce the new PAYGO requirement for direct spending and revenue legislation. Generally, the new statutory PAYGO process provides that if the net effect of direct spending and revenue legislation enacted during a year increases the deficit, budgetary resources in certain direct spending programs are cut in order to eliminate the increase in the deficit. Specifically, the average budgetary effects (i.e., any increase or decrease in the deficit) over five- and 10-year periods[2] of each direct spending and revenue act are placed on five- and 10-year scorecards, respectively. Like the PAYGO process under the BEA, the sequestration process is triggered by a report from the OMB director issued 14 days after Congress adjourns at the end of a session. If either scorecard shows a positive balance (referred to as a debit) for the budget year, the President is required to issue a sequestration order cancelling budgetary resources in non-exempt direct spending programs sufficient to eliminate the balance (the larger balance if both scorecards show a positive balance).[3]

SPENDING LEGISLATION

The spending policies of the budget resolution generally are implemented through two different types of spending legislation. Policies involving discretionary spending are implemented in the context of annual appropriations acts, whereas policies affecting direct or mandatory spending (which, for the most part, involves entitlement programs) are carried out in substantive legislation.

All discretionary spending is under the jurisdiction of the House and Senate Appropriations Committees. Direct spending is under the jurisdiction of the various legislative committees of the House and Senate; the House Ways and Means Committee and the Senate Finance Committee have the largest shares of direct spending jurisdiction. (Some entitlement programs, such as Medicaid, are funded in annual appropriations acts, but such spending is not considered to be discretionary.) The enforcement procedures under the congressional budget process, mentioned above, apply equally to discretionary and direct spending.

Authorizing Measures

The rules of the House and (to a lesser extent) the Senate require that agencies and programs be authorized in law before an appropriation is made for them. An authorizing act is a law that (1) establishes a program or agency and the terms and conditions under which it operates; and (2) authorizes the enactment of appropriations for that program or agency. Authorizing legislation may originate in either the House or the Senate and may be considered any time during the year. Many agencies and programs have temporary authorizations that have to be renewed annually or every few years.

Action on appropriations measures sometimes is delayed by the failure of Congress to enact necessary authorizing legislation. The House and Senate often waive or disregard their rules against unauthorized appropriations for ongoing programs that have not yet been reauthorized.

The budgetary impact of authorizing legislation depends on whether it contains only discretionary authorizations (for which funding is provided in annual appropriations acts) or direct spending, which itself enables an agency to enter into obligations.

The Annual Appropriations Process

An appropriations act is a law passed by Congress that provides federal agencies legal authority to incur obligations and the Treasury Department authority to make payments for designated purposes. The power of appropriation derives from the Constitution, which in Article I, Section 9, provides that "[n]o money shall be drawn from the Treasury but in consequence of appropriations made by law." The power to appropriate is exclusively a legislative power; it functions as a limitation on the executive branch. An agency may not spend more than the amount appropriated to it, and it may use available funds only for the purposes and according to the conditions provided by Congress.

The Constitution does not require annual appropriations, but since the First Congress the practice has been to make appropriations for a single fiscal year. Appropriations must be used (obligated) in the fiscal year for which they are provided, unless the law provides that they shall be available for a longer period of time. All provisions in an appropriations act, such as limitations on the use of funds, expire at the end of the fiscal year, unless the language of the act extends their period of effectiveness.

The President requests annual appropriations in his budget submitted each year. In support of the President's appropriations requests, agencies submit justification materials to the House and Senate Appropriations Committees. These materials provide considerably more detail than is contained in the

President's budget and are used in support of agency testimony during Appropriations subcommittee hearings on the President's budget.

Congress passes three main types of appropriations measures. *Regular appropriations* acts provide budget authority to agencies for the next fiscal year. *Supplemental appropriations* acts provide additional budget authority during the current fiscal year when the regular appropriation is insufficient or to finance activities not provided for in the regular appropriation. *Continuing appropriations* acts provide stop-gap (or full-year) funding for agencies that have not received a regular appropriation.

In a typical session, Congress acts on 12 regular appropriations bills and at least two supplemental appropriations measures. Because of recurring delays in the appropriations process, Congress also typically passes one or more continuing appropriations each year. The scope and duration of these measures depend on the status of the regular appropriations bills and the degree of budgetary conflict between the President and Congress. In recent years, Congress has merged two or more of the regular appropriations acts for a fiscal year into a single, omnibus appropriations act.

By precedent, appropriations originate in the House of Representatives. In the House, appropriations measures are originated by the Appropriations Committee (when it marks up or reports the measure) rather than being introduced by a Member beforehand. Before the full Committee acts on the bill, it is considered in the relevant Appropriations subcommittee (the House and Senate Appropriations Committees have 12 parallel subcommittees). The House subcommittees typically hold extensive hearings on appropriations requests shortly after the President's budget is submitted. In marking up their appropriations bills, the various subcommittees are guided by the discretionary spending limits and the allocations made to them under Section 302 of the 1974 Congressional Budget Act.

The Senate usually considers appropriations measures after they have been passed by the House. When House action on appropriations bills is delayed, however, the Senate sometimes expedites its actions by considering a Senate-numbered bill up to the stage of final passage. Upon receipt of the House-passed bill in the Senate, it is amended with the text that the Senate already has agreed to (as a single amendment) and then passed by the Senate. Hearings in the Senate Appropriations subcommittees generally are not as extensive as those held by counterpart subcommittees in the House.

The basic unit of an appropriation is an account. A single unnumbered paragraph in an appropriations act comprises one account and all provisions of that paragraph pertain to that account and to no other, unless the text expressly gives them broader scope. Any provision limiting the use of funds enacted in that paragraph is a restriction on that account alone.

Over the years, appropriations have been consolidated into a relatively small number of accounts. It is typical for a federal agency to have a single account for all its expenses of operation and additional accounts for other purposes such as construction. Accordingly, most appropriation accounts encompass a number of activities or projects. The appropriation sometimes earmarks specific amounts to particular activities within the account, but the more common practice is to provide detailed information on the amounts intended for each activity in other sources (principally, the committee reports accompanying the measures).

In addition to the substantive limitations (and other provisions) associated with each account, each appropriations act has "general provisions" that apply to all of the accounts in a title or in the whole act. These general provisions appear as numbered sections, usually at the end of the title or the act.

The standard appropriation is for a single fiscal year—the funds have to be obligated during the fiscal year for which they are provided; they lapse if not obligated by the end of that year. An appropriation that does not mention the period during which the funds are to be available is a one- year appropriation. Congress also makes no-year appropriations by specifying that the funds shall remain available until expended. No-year funds are carried over to future years, even if they have not been obligated. Congress sometimes makes multiyear appropriations, which provide for funds to be available for two or more fiscal years.

Appropriations measures also contain other types of provisions that serve specialized purposes. These include provisions that liquidate (pay off) obligations made pursuant to certain contract authority; reappropriate funds provided in previous years; transfer funds from one account to another; rescind funds (or release deferred funds); or set ceilings on the amount of obligations that can be made under permanent appropriations, on the amount of direct or guaranteed loans that can be made, or on the amount of administrative expenses that can be incurred during the fiscal year. In addition to providing funds, appropriations acts often contain substantive limitations on government agencies.

Detailed information on how funds are to be spent, along with other directives or guidance, is provided in the reports accompanying the various appropriations measures. Agencies ordinarily abide by report language in spending the funds appropriated by Congress.

The appropriations reports do not comment on every item of expenditure. Report language is most likely when the Appropriations Committee prefers to spend more or less on a particular item than the President has requested or when the committee wants to earmark funds for a particular project or activity. When a particular item is mentioned by the committee, there is a strong expectation that the agency will adhere to the instructions.

REVENUE LEGISLATION

Article I, Section 8 of the Constitution gives Congress the power to levy "taxes, duties, imposts, and excises." Section 7 of this article requires that all revenue measures originate in the House of Representatives.

In the House, revenue legislation is under the jurisdiction of the Ways and Means Committee; in the Senate, jurisdiction is held by the Finance Committee. While House rules bar other committees from reporting revenue legislation, sometimes another committee will report legislation levying user fees on a class that benefits from a particular service or program or that is being regulated by a federal agency. In many of these cases, the user fee legislation is referred subsequently to the Ways and Means Committee.

Most revenues derive from existing provisions of the tax code or Social Security law, which continue in effect from year to year unless changed by Congress. This tax structure can be expected to produce increasing amounts of revenue in future years as the economy expands and incomes rise. Nevertheless, Congress usually makes some changes in the tax laws each year, either to raise or lower revenues or to redistribute the tax burden.

Congress typically acts on revenue legislation pursuant to proposals in the President's budget. An early step in congressional work on revenue legislation is publication by CBO of its own estimates (developed in consultation with the Joint Tax Committee) of the revenue impact of the President's budget proposals. The congressional estimates often differ significantly from those presented in the President's budget.

The revenue totals in the budget resolution establish the framework for subsequent action on revenue measures. The budget resolution contains only revenue totals and total recommended changes; it does not allocate these totals among revenue sources (although it does set out Medicare receipts separately), nor does it specify which provisions of the tax code are to be changed.

The House and Senate often consider major revenue measures, such as the Tax Reform Act of 1986, under their regular legislative procedures. However, as has been the case with direct spending programs, many of the most significant changes in revenue policy in recent years have been made in the context of the reconciliation process. Although revenue changes usually are incorporated into omnibus budget reconciliation measures, along with spending changes (and sometimes debt-limit increases), revenue reconciliation legislation may be considered on a separate legislative track (e.g., the Tax Equity and Fiscal Responsibility Act of 1982).

When the reconciliation process is used to advance revenue reductions (or spending increases) that would lead to a deficit, or would enlarge an existing deficit, Section 313 of the 1974 Congressional Budget Act (referred to as the Senate's "Byrd rule") limits the legislative changes to the period covered by the reconciliation directives. Accordingly, some recent tax cuts have been subject to sunset dates.

In enacting revenue legislation, Congress often establishes or alters tax expenditures. The term "tax expenditures" is defined in the 1974 Congressional Budget Act to include revenue losses due to deductions, exemptions, credits, and other exceptions to the basic tax structure. Tax expenditures are a means by which the federal government pursues public policy objectives and can be regarded as alternatives to other policy instruments such as grants or loans. The Joint Tax Committee estimates the revenue effects of legislation changing tax expenditures, and it also publishes five-year projections of these provisions as an annual committee print.

DEBT-LIMIT LEGISLATION

When the revenues collected by the federal government are not sufficient to cover its expenditures, it must finance the shortfall through borrowing. Federal borrowing is subject to a public debt limit established by statute. When the federal government operates with a budget deficit, the public debt limit must be increased periodically. The frequency of congressional action to raise the debt limit has ranged in the past from several times in one year to once in several years. When the federal government incurred large and growing surpluses in recent years, Congress did not have to increase the debt limit, but the enactment of increases in the debt limit has again become necessary with the recurrence of deficits.

Legislation to raise the public debt limit falls under the jurisdiction of the House Ways and Means Committee and the Senate Finance Committee. Although consideration of such measures in the House usually is constrained through the use of special rules, Senate action sometimes is far- ranging with regard to the issues covered. In the past, the Senate has added many non-germane provisions to debt-limit measures, such as the 1985 Balanced Budget Act.

In 1979, the House amended its rules to provide for the automatic engrossment of a measure increasing the debt limit upon final adoption of the conference report on the budget resolution. The rule, House Rule XLIX (commonly referred to as the Gephardt rule), was intended to facilitate quick action on debt increases. However, the Senate had no comparable rule. For years, the House and Senate could enact debt-limit legislation originating under the Gephardt rule or arising under conventional legislative procedures. During the past decade, Congress has enacted debt-limit increases as part of omnibus budget reconciliation measures, continuing appropriations acts, and other legislation. The House recodified the Gephardt rule as House Rule XXIII at the beginning of the 106th Congress, repealed it at the beginning of the 107th Congress, and reinstated it, as new Rule XXVII, at the beginning of the 108th Congress.

RECONCILIATION LEGISLATION

Beginning in 1980, Congress has used reconciliation legislation to implement many of its most significant budget policies. Section 310 of the 1974 Congressional Budget Act sets forth a special procedure for the development and consideration of reconciliation legislation. Reconciliation legislation is used by Congress to bring existing revenue and spending law into conformity with the policies in the budget resolution. Reconciliation is an optional process, but Congress has used it more years than not; during the period covering 1980 through 2010, 20 reconciliation measures were enacted into law and three were vetoed.

The reconciliation process has two stages—the adoption of reconciliation instructions in the budget resolution and the enactment of reconciliation legislation that implements changes in revenue or spending laws. Although reconciliation has been used since 1980, specific procedures tend to vary from year to year.

Reconciliation is used to change the amount of revenues, budget authority, or outlays generated by existing law. In a few instances, reconciliation has been used to adjust the public debt limit. On the spending side, the process focuses on entitlement laws; it may not be used, however, to impel changes in Social Security law. Reconciliation sometimes has been applied to discretionary authorizations (which are funded in annual appropriations acts), but this is not the usual practice.

Reconciliation was used in the 1980s and into the 1990s as a deficit-reduction tool. Beginning in the latter part of the 1990s, some reconciliation measures were used principally to reduce revenues, thereby increasing the deficit. At the beginning of the 110th Congress, both chambers adopted rules requiring that reconciliation be used solely for deficit reduction.

Reconciliation Directives

Reconciliation begins with a directive in a budget resolution instructing designated committees to report legislation changing existing law or pending legislation. These instructions have three components: (1) they name the committee (or committees) that are directed to report legislation; (2)they specify the amounts by which existing laws are to be changed (but do not identify how these changes are to be made, which laws are to be altered, or the programs to be affected); and (3) they usually set a deadline by which the designated committees are to recommend the changes in law. The instructions typically cover the same fiscal years covered by the budget resolution. Sometimes, budget resolutions have provided for more than one reconciliation measure to be considered during a session.

The dollar amounts are computed with reference to the CBO baseline. Thus, a change represents the amount by which revenues or spending would decrease or increase from baseline levels as a result of changes made in existing law. This computation is itself based on assumptions about the future level of revenues or spending under current law (or policy) and about the dollar changes that would ensue from new legislation. Hence, the savings associated with the reconciliation process are assumed savings. The actual changes in revenues or spending may differ from those estimated when the reconciliation instructions are formulated.

Although the instructions do not mention the programs to be changed, they are based on assumptions as to the savings or deficit reduction (or, in some cases, increases) that would result from particular changes in revenue provisions or spending programs. These program assumptions are sometimes printed in the reports on the budget resolution. Even when the assumptions are not published, committees and Members usually have a good idea of the specific program changes contemplated by the reconciliation instructions.

A committee has discretion to decide on the legislative changes to be recommended. It is not bound by the program changes recommended or assumed by the Budget Committees in the reports accompanying the budget resolution. Further, a committee has to recommend legislation estimated to produce dollar changes for each category delineated in the instructions to it.

When a budget resolution containing a reconciliation instruction has been approved by Congress, the instruction has the status of an order by the House and Senate to designated committees to recommend legislation, usually by a date certain. It is expected that committees will carry out the instructions of their parent chamber, but the 1974 Congressional Budget Act does not provide any sanctions against committees that fail to do so.

Development and Consideration of Reconciliation Measures

When more than one committee in the House and Senate is subject to reconciliation directives, the proposed legislative changes usually are consolidated by the Budget Committees into an omnibus bill. The 1974 Congressional Budget Act does not permit the Budget Committees to revise substantively the legislation recommended by the committees of jurisdiction. This restriction pertains even when the Budget Committees estimate that the proposed legislation will fall short of the dollar changes called for in the instructions. Sometimes, the Budget Committees, working with the leadership, develop alternatives to the committee recommendations, to be offered as floor amendments, so as to achieve greater compliance with the reconciliation directives.

The 1974 act requires that amendments offered to reconciliation legislation in either the House or the Senate be deficit neutral. To meet this requirement, an amendment reducing revenues or increasing spending must offset these deficit increases by equivalent revenue increases or spending cuts.

During the first several years' experience with reconciliation, the legislation contained many provisions that were extraneous to the purpose of reducing the deficit. The reconciliation submissions of committees included such things as provisions that had no budgetary effect, that increased spending or reduced revenues, or that violated another committee's jurisdiction.

In 1985, the Senate adopted a rule (commonly referred to as the Byrd rule) on a temporary basis as a means of curbing these practices. The Byrd rule has been extended and modified several times over the years. In 1990, the Byrd rule was incorporated into the 1974 Congressional Budget Act as Section 313 and made permanent.

Although the House has no rule comparable to the Senate's Byrd rule, it may use other devices to control the inclusion of extraneous matter in reconciliation legislation. In particular, the House may use special rules to make in order amendments that strike such matter.

House and Senate Earmark Disclosure Rules

In 2007, both the House and Senate adopted rules intended to bring more transparency to the process surrounding earmarks. Although the definitions vary, an earmark generally is considered to be an allocation of resources to specifically-targeted beneficiaries, either through discretionary or direct spending, limited tax benefits, or limited tariff benefits.[4]

Concern about earmarking practices arose over such provisions being inserted into legislation or accompanying reports without any identification of the sponsor, and the belief that many earmarks were not subject to proper scrutiny and diverted resources to lesser-priority items or items without sufficient justification, thereby contributing to wasteful spending or revenue loss.

In response to this concern, earmark rules were adopted that vary by chamber, but include three main features. The first feature is a requirement that Members requesting a congressional earmark provide a written statement to the chair and ranking minority member of the committee of jurisdiction that includes the Member's name, the name and address of the intended earmark recipient, the purpose of the earmark, and a certification that the Member or Member's spouse has no financial interest in such an earmark. (The Senate rule applies not only to the spouse but the entire immediate family.)

The second feature is a general requirement that committees provide a list of all earmarks included in reported legislation. The third feature is a point of order against legislation that is not accompanied by a list of included earmarks. These vary by chamber.

House of Representatives

House Rule XXI, clause 9, generally requires that certain types of measures be accompanied by a list of earmarks or a statement that the measure contains no earmarks.[5] If the list of earmarks or the statement that no earmark exists in the measure is absent, a point of order may lie against the measure's floor consideration. The point of order applies to the absence of such a list or statement, and does not speak to the completeness or the accuracy of such document.

House earmark disclosure rules apply to any congressional earmark included in either the text of the measure or the committee report accompanying the measure, as well as the conference report and joint explanatory statement. The disclosure requirements apply to items in authorizing, appropriations, and revenue legislation. Furthermore, they apply not only to measures reported by committees, but also to unreported measures, "manager's amendments," Senate measures, and conference reports.

These earmark disclosure requirements, however, do not apply to all legislation at all times. Not subject to the rule are floor amendments (except a "manager's amendment"), amendments between the Houses, or amendments considered as adopted under a self-executing special rule, including a committee amendment in the nature of a substitute made in order as original text. The earmark rule, as with most House rules, is not self enforcing and relies instead on a Member raising a point of order if the rule is violated. When a measure is considered under suspension of the rules, House rules are laid aside and earmark disclosure rules are, therefore, waived. It is not in order to consider a special rule that waives earmark requirements under the House rule.

The Senate

Senate Rule XLIV creates a point of order against a motion to proceed to consider a measure or a vote on adoption of a conference report, unless the chair of the committee or the Majority Leader (or designee) certifies that a complete list of earmarks and the name of each Senator requesting each earmark is available on a publicly accessible congressional website in a searchable form at least 48 hours before the vote. If a Senator proposes a floor amendment containing an earmark, those items must be printed in the *Congressional Record* as soon as "practicable."[6] If the earmark certification requirements have not been met, a point of order may lie against consideration of the measure or a vote on the conference report. The point of order applies only to the absence of such certification, and does not speak to its accuracy.

Senate earmark disclosure rules apply to any congressional earmark included in either the text of the bill or a committee report accompanying the bill, as well as a conference report and joint explanatory statement. The disclosure requirements apply to items in authorizing, appropriations, and revenue legislation. Furthermore, they apply not only to measures reported by committees, but also to unreported measures, amendments, House bills, and conference reports.

The earmark rule may be waived either by unanimous consent or by motion, which requires the affirmative vote of three-fifths of all Senators (60, if there are no vacancies).[7] The earmark rule, as with most Senate rules, is not self enforcing and relies instead on a Senator raising a point of order if the rule is violated.

IMPOUNDMENT AND LINE-ITEM VETO

Impoundment

Although an appropriation limits the amounts that can be spent, it also establishes the expectation that the available funds will be used to carry out authorized activities. Therefore, when an agency fails to use all or part of an appropriation, it deviates from the intentions of Congress. The Impoundment Control Act of 1974 prescribes rules and procedures for instances in which available funds are impounded.

An impoundment is an action or inaction by the President or a federal agency that delays or withholds the obligation or expenditure of budget authority provided in law. The 1974 Impoundment Control Act divides impoundments into two categories and establishes distinct procedures for each. A *deferral* delays the use of funds; a *rescission* is a presidential request that Congress rescind (cancel) an appropriation or other form of budget authority. Deferral and rescission are exclusive and comprehensive categories; an impoundment is either a rescission or a deferral—it cannot be both or something else.

Although impoundments are defined broadly by the 1974 act, in practice they are limited to major actions that affect the level or rate of expenditure. As a general practice, only deliberate curtailments of expenditure are reported as impoundments; actions having other purposes that incidently affect the rate of spending are not recorded as impoundments. For example, if an agency were to delay the award of a contract because of a dispute with a vendor, the delay would not be an impoundment; if the delay were for the purpose of reducing an expenditure, it would be an impoundment. The line between routine administrative actions and impoundments is not clear and controversy occasionally arises as to whether a particular action constitutes an impoundment.

Rescissions

To propose a rescission, the President must submit a message to Congress specifying the amount to be rescinded, the accounts and programs involved, the estimated fiscal and program effects, and the reasons for the rescission. Multiple rescissions can be grouped in a single message. After the message has been submitted to it, Congress has 45 days of "continuous session" (usually a larger number of calendar days) during which it can pass a rescission bill. Congress may rescind all, part, or none of the amount proposed by the President.

If Congress does not approve a rescission in legislation by the expiration of this period, the President must make the funds available for obligation and expenditure. If the President fails to release funds at the expiration of the 45-day period for proposed rescissions, the comptroller general may bring suit to compel their release. This has been a rare occurrence, however.

Deferrals

To defer funds, the President submits a message to Congress setting forth the amount, the affected account and program, the reasons for the deferral, the estimated fiscal and program effects, and the period of time during which the funds are to be deferred. The President may not propose a deferral for a period of time beyond the end of the fiscal year, nor may he propose a deferral that would cause the funds to lapse or otherwise prevent an agency from spending appropriated funds prudently. In accounts where unobligated funds remain available beyond the fiscal year, the President may defer the funds again in the next fiscal year.

At present, the President may defer only for the reasons set forth in the Antideficiency Act, including to provide for contingencies, to achieve savings made possible by or through changes in requirements or greater efficiency of operations, and as specifically provided by law. He may not defer funds for policy reasons (for example, to curtail overall federal spending or because he is opposed to a particular program).

The comptroller general reviews all proposed rescissions and deferrals and advises Congress of their legality and possible budgetary and program effects. The comptroller general also notifies Congress of any rescission or deferral not reported by the President and may reclassify an improperly classified impoundment. In all cases, a notification to Congress by the comptroller general has the same legal effect as an impoundment message of the President.

The 1974 Impoundment Control Act provides for special types of legislation—rescission bills and deferral resolutions—for Congress to use in exercising its impoundment control powers. However, pursuant to court decisions that held the legislative veto to be unconstitutional, Congress may not use deferral resolutions to disapprove a deferral. Further, Congress has been reluctant to use rescission bills regularly. Congress, instead, usually acts on impoundment matters within the framework of the annual appropriations measures.

Line-Item Veto

During the 104th Congress, the Line Item Veto Act (P.L. 104-130) was enacted as an amendment to the 1974 Impoundment Control Act. The Supreme Court ruled the Line Item Veto Act unconstitutional in June 1998.

The authority granted to the President under the Line Item Veto Act differed markedly from the veto authority available to most chief executives at the state level. First, the President could not veto individual parts of legislation submitted for his approval. Under normal constitutional procedures, the President must approve or veto any measure in its entirety. His authority to use the line-item veto came into play only after a measure had been signed into law. Second, this authority applied not only to annual appropriations, but extended to new entitlement spending and targeted tax benefits as well. The line-item veto authority was intended to be in effect for eight years, from the beginning of 1997 through the end of 2004.

The Line Item Veto Act reversed the presumption underlying the process for the consideration of rescissions under the 1974 Impoundment Control Act. Under the Line Item Veto Act, presidential proposals would take effect unless overturned by legislative action. The act authorized the President to identify at enactment individual items in legislation that he proposed not go into effect. The identification was based not just upon the statutory language, but on the entire legislative history and documentation. The President had to notify Congress promptly of his proposals and provide supporting information. Congress had to respond within a limited period of time by enacting a law if it wanted to disapprove the President's proposals; otherwise, they would take effect permanently.

President Clinton exercised the line-item veto authority several times during the 1997 session before the act was declared unconstitutional.

ACKNOWLEDGMENTS

This chapter was originally written by Robert Keith, formerly a Specialist in American National Government at CRS, and Allen Schick, formerly a Consultant at CRS. The analysts listed on the cover of this chapter, and under the "author contact information," updated portions of the report and are available to answer questions related to the federal budget process.

End Notes

[1] For more detailed information on the statutory requirement, see CRS Report R41 157, *The Statutory Pay-As-You-Go Act of 2010: Summary and Legislative History*, by Bill Heniff Jr.

[2] The five-year period covers the budget year and four fiscal years thereafter, and the 10-year period covers the budget year and nine fiscal years thereafter. The statutory rule also requires that any budgetary effects for the current year must be added to the budgetary effects for the budget year.

[3] Most direct spending programs and activities, including Social Security benefits, veterans' programs, retirement and disability benefits, and low-income programs, among others, are exempt from any sequestration. In addition, the amount of any sequestration is limited to 4% for Medicare and 2% for certain health and medical care activities.

[4] For more information on House and Senate earmark rules, see CRS Report RL34462, *House and Senate Procedural Rules Concerning Earmark Disclosure*, by Sandy Streeter.

[5] Depending upon the type of measure, the list or statement is to be included either in the measure's accompanying report, or printed in the *Congressional Record*.

[6] The rule does not apply to all earmarks in floor amendments, only those "not included in the bill or joint resolution as placed on the calendar or as reported by any committee, in a committee report on such a bill or joint resolution, or a committee report of the Senate on a companion measure," as stated in Rule XLIV, paragraph 4(a).

[7] These points of order may also be waived if the Majority and Minority Leaders jointly agree that "such a waiver is necessary as a result of a significant disruption to Senate facilities or to the availability of the Internet." Senate Rule XLIV, paragraph 12.

In: United States Federal Budget Process ISBN: 978-1-61209-844-9
Editors: Gerard T. Brenner et al.

Chapter 2

POINTS OF ORDER IN THE CONGRESSIONAL BUDGET PROCESS

James V. Saturno

SUMMARY

The Congressional Budget Act of 1974 (Titles I-IX of P.L. 93-344, as amended) created a process that Congress uses each year to establish and enforce the parameters for budgetary legislation. Enforcement of budgetary decisions is accomplished through the use of points of order, and through the reconciliation process. Points of order are prohibitions against certain types of legislation or congressional actions. These prohibitions are enforced when a Member raises a point of order against legislation that may violate these rules when it is considered by the House or Senate.

This chapter summarizes points of order under the Congressional Budget Act of 1974, as amended, and related points of order established in the budget resolutions adopted by Congress in 2007 (S.Con.Res. 21, 110th Congress), 2008 (S.Con.Res. 70, 110th Congress), and 2009 (S.Con.Res. 13, 111th Congress), as well as the Rules of the House for the 111th Congress, the Budget Enforcement Act of 1990 (P.L. 10 1-508), and the Statutory Pay-As-You-Go Act of 2010 (P.L. 111-139). In addition, it describes how points of order are applied and the processes used for their waiver in the House and Senate.

INTRODUCTION

The Congressional Budget Act of 1974[1] established the basic framework that is used today for congressional consideration of budget and fiscal policy. The act provided for the adoption of a concurrent resolution on the budget (budget resolution) as a mechanism for coordinating congressional budgetary decision making. This process supplements other House and Senate procedures for considering spending and revenue legislation by allowing Congress to establish and enforce parameters with which those separate pieces of budgetary legislation must be consistent. The parameters are established each year when Congress adopts the budget resolution, setting forth overall levels for new budget authority, outlays, revenues, deficit, and debt.

These overall spending levels are then allocated to the various committees in the House and Senate responsible for spending legislation. The overall levels and allocations are then enforced through the use of points of order, and through implementing legislation, such as that enacted through the reconciliation process.[2] Points of order are prohibitions against certain types of legislation or congressional actions. These prohibitions are enforced when a Member raises a point of order against legislation that is alleged to violate these rules when it is considered by the House or Senate. Points of order are not self-enforcing. A point of order must be raised by a Member on the floor of the chamber before the presiding officer can rule on its application, and thus for its enforcement.

Although the congressional budget process encompasses myriad procedures dealing with spending, revenue, and debt legislation, this chapter focuses only on that portion of the process that stems from the Congressional Budget Act. The tables below list the points of order currently included in the Congressional Budget Act (Table 1), as well as related points of order established in other measures. These other measures include the FY20 10 budget resolution (Table 2); FY2009 budget resolution (Table 3); the FY2008 budget resolution (Table 4); the rules of the House as adopted under H.Res. 5, 111th Congress (Table 5); the Budget Enforcement Act of 1990 (Table 6); and the Statutory Pay-As-You-Go Act of 2010 (Table 7) that pertain to the consideration, contents, implementation, or enforcement of budgetary decisions.

Points of order are typically in the form of a provision stating that "it shall not be in order" for the House or Senate to take a specified action or consider certain legislation that is inconsistent with the requirements of the Budget Act. Other provisions of the act, formulated differently, establish various requirements or procedures, particularly concerning the contents and consideration of the budget resolution or reconciliation legislation. These provisions, however, are not typically enforced through points of order, and are not included here.[3]

As amended through the Balanced Budget Act of 1997, points of order in the Congressional Budget Act are permanent. None of the provisions listed in Table 1 is scheduled to expire, although several points of order have limited applicability or have been rendered moot by the expiration of limits they were intended to enforce.[4] The freestanding point of order protecting the Social Security trust fund in the House established in the Budget Enforcement Act (see Table 6) is also permanent. However, other points of order established under recent budget resolutions have various sunset provisions or limited application (see Table 3 and Table 4 for examples).

APPLICATION OF POINTS OF ORDER

Most points of order in the Budget Act apply to measures as a whole, as well as to motions, amendments, or conference reports to those measures. When a point of order is sustained against consideration of some matter, the effect is that the matter in question falls.

The application of points of order in the House is clarified in Section 315 of the Budget Act. This provision states that for cases in which a reported measure is considered pursuant to a special rule, a point of order against a bill "as reported" would apply to the text made in order by the rule as original text for the purpose of amendment or to the text on which the previous question is ordered directly to passage. In this way, no point of order would be considered as applying (and no waiver would be required) if a substitute resolved the problem. In addition, the Rules of the House for the 111th Congress include a provision further specifying that for measures considered pursuant to a special rule, points of order under Title III of the Budget Act apply without regard to whether the measure considered is actually that reported from committee. Under Rule XXI, clause 8, points of order apply to the form of a measure recommended by the reporting committee where the statute uses the term "as reported" (in the case of a measure that has been reported), the form of the measure made in order as an original text for the purpose of amendment, or the form of the measure on which the previous question is ordered directly to passage.

The effect of a point of order in the Senate is clarified under Section 312(f), which provides that when a point of order against a measure is sustained, the measure is recommitted to the appropriate committee for any further consideration. This allows the Senate an opportunity to remedy the problem that caused the point of order. Section 312(d) is also designed to provide the Senate with the opportunity to remedy a problem that would provoke a point of order. This provision states that a point of order may not be raised against a measure, amendment, motion, or conference report while an amendment or motion that would remedy the problem is pending.

Section 312(e) clarifies that any point of order that would apply in the Senate against an amendment also applies against amendments between the houses. Further, this section also states that the effect would "be the same as if the Senate had disagreed to the amendment." This would allow the Senate to keep the underlying measure pending, and thus retain the ability to resolve their differences with the House. This provision therefore means that any resolution of the differences between the House- and Senate-passed versions of a measure, whether it is in the form of a conference report or not, must adhere to the provisions of the Budget Act.

There are exceptions to the general principle of applying points of order to a measure as a whole. The most salient is probably Section 313, the so-called Byrd Rule. This section applies to matter "contained in any title or provision" in a reconciliation bill or resolution (or conference report thereon), as well as any amendment or motion. If a point of order is sustained under this section, only the provision in question is stricken, or the amendment or motion falls.[5] Several of the points of order in the Senate established under recent budget resolutions have been written so that they apply to individual provisions rather than the measure as a whole, in the manner provided in Section 313(e) of the Budget Act. The point of order against emergency spending designations (Section 403(e)(1) of S.Con.Res. 13 (11 1th Congress)) further provides that, if sustained, the effect of this point of order is that a provision making an emergency designation shall be stricken, and may not be offered as an amendment from the floor.

Table 1. Points of Order Under the Congressional Budget Act of 1974

Section	Description	Application	Senate Waiver Votea
301(g)	In the Senate, prohibits consideration of a budget resolution using more than one set of economic assumptions.	Budget resolution, amendment, or conference report.	Simple majority
301(i)	In the Senate, prohibits consideration of a budget resolution that would decrease the Social Security surplus in any fiscal year covered by the resolution.	Budget resolution, amendment, motion, or conference report.	Three-fifths*
302(c)	Prohibits the consideration of any measure within the jurisdiction of the House or Senate Appropriations Committees that provides new budget authority for a fiscal year until the committee makes the suballocation required by Section 302(b).	Bill, joint resolution, amendment, motion, or conference report.	Three-fifths*
302(f)(1)	In the House, after action on a budget resolution is completed, prohibits consideration of legislation providing new budget authority for any fiscal year that would cause the applicable allocation of new budget authority made pursuant to Section 302(a) or (b) for the first fiscal year or for the total of all fiscal years to be exceeded.[b,c]	Bill, joint resolution, amendment, or conference report.	n/a
302(f)(2)(A)	In the Senate, after a budget resolution is agreed to, prohibits consideration of legislation (from any committee other than the Appropriations Committee) that would cause the applicable allocation of new budget authority or outlays made pursuant to Section 302(a) for the first fiscal year or for the total of all fiscal years to be exceeded.	Bill, joint resolution, amendment, motion, or conference report.	Three-fifths*
302(f)(2)(B)	In the Senate, after a budget resolution has been agreed to, prohibits consideration of legislation from the Appropriations Committee that would cause the applicable suballocation of new budget authority or outlays made pursuant to Section 302(b) to be exceeded.	Bill, joint resolution, amendment, motion, or conference report.	Three-fifths*

Table 1 (Continued)

Section	Description	Application	Senate Waiver Votea
303(a)	Prohibits consideration of legislation providing new budget authority, an increase or decrease in revenues, an increase or decrease in the public debt limit, new entitlement authority (in the Senate only), or an increase or decrease in outlays (in the Senate only) for a fiscal year until a concurrent resolution for that fiscal year has been agreed to.[b,d]	Bill, joint resolution, amendment, motion, or conference report.	Simple majoritye
303(c)	In the Senate, prohibits consideration of any appropriations measure until a concurrent resolution for that fiscal year has been agreed to, and an allocation has been made to the Committee on Appropriations under Section 302(a).[d]	Bill, joint resolution, amendment or conference report.	Simple majoritye
305(b)(2)	In the Senate, prohibits consideration of nongermane amendments.[f]	Amendment.	Three-fifths
305(c)(4)	In the Senate, prohibits consideration of nongermane amendments to amendments in disagreement to a budget resolution (Section 310(e) applies this prohibition to amendments in disagreement to reconciliation legislation as well).	Amendment in disagreement to a budget resolution (or to reconciliation legislation).	Three-fifths
305(d)	In the Senate, prohibits a vote on a budget resolution unless the figures contained in the resolution are mathematically consistent.	Budget resolution or conference report.	Simple majority
306	Prohibits consideration of matters within the jurisdiction of the House or Senate Budget Committee except when it is a measure reported by the committee, or the committee is discharged from further consideration of the measure, or an amendment to such a measure.[g]	Bill, resolution, amendment, motion, or conference report.	Three-fifths
309	In the House, prohibits consideration of an adjournment resolution for more than three calendar days during July until the House has approved all regular appropriations bills for the upcoming fiscal year.	Resolution.	n/a
310(d)	Prohibits the consideration of amendments to reconciliation legislation that would increase the deficit either by increasing outlays or reducing	Amendment.	Three-fifths

Table 1 (Continued)

Section	Description	Application	Senate Waiver Votea
	revenues, except that in the Senate a motion to strike a provision shall always be in order.[h]		
310(e)	In the Senate, prohibits consideration of nongermane amendments to reconciliation legislation or to amendments in disagreement to reconciliation (by reference to Sections 305(b)(2) and 305(c)(4)).	Amendment.	Three-fifths
310(f)	In the House, prohibits consideration of an adjournment resolution of more than three calendar days during July until the House has completed action on any required reconciliation legislation.	Resolution.	n/a
310(g)	Prohibits the consideration of reconciliation legislation that contains recommendations with respect to Social Security.	Bill, joint resolution, amendment, motion, or conference report.	Three-fifths*
311(a)(1)	In the House, prohibits consideration of legislation that would cause new budget authority or outlays to exceed or revenues to fall below the levels set forth in the budget resolution for the first fiscal year or for the total of all fiscal years for which allocations are made pursuant to Section 302(a)b,i	Bill, joint resolution, amendment, motion, or conference report.	n/a
311(a)(2)	In the Senate, prohibits consideration of legislation that would cause new budget authority or outlays to exceed the levels set forth in the budget resolution for the first fiscal year, or revenues to fall below the levels set forth in the budget resolution for the first fiscal year or for the total of all fiscal years for which allocations are made pursuant to Section 302(a).	Bill, joint resolution, amendment, motion, or conference report.	Three-fifths*
311(a)(3)	In the Senate, prohibits consideration of legislation that would cause a decrease in Social Security surpluses or an increase in Social Security deficits relative to the level set forth in the budget resolution for the first	Bill, joint resolution, amendment, motion, or conference report.	Three-fifths*

Table 1 (Continued)

Section	Description	Application	Senate Waiver Votea
	fiscal year or for the total of all fiscal years for which allocations are made pursuant to Section 302(a).		
312(b)	In the Senate, prohibits the consideration of legislation that would cause any of the discretionary spending limits specified in Section 251(c) of the Balanced Budget and Emergency Deficit Control Act of 1985, as amended, to be exceeded.[j]	Bill, joint resolution, amendment, motion, or conference report.	Three-fifths*
312(c)	In the Senate, prohibits consideration of a budget resolution that provides for a deficit in excess of the maximum deficit amount specified in the Balanced Budget and Emergency Deficit Control Act of 1985, as amended, for the first fiscal year set forth in the resolution.[k]	Budget resolution, amendment, or conference report.	Three-fifths*
313	In the Senate prohibits consideration of extraneous provisions in reconciliation legislation.[l]	Reconciliation bill or resolution (any title or provision), amendment, motion, or conference report.	Three-fifths
401(a)	Prohibits consideration of legislation providing new contract authority, borrowing authority, or credit authority not limited to amounts provided in appropriations acts.[m]	Bill, joint resolution, amendment, motion, or conference report.	Simple majority
401(b)	Prohibits consideration of legislation providing new entitlement authority that is to become effective during the current fiscal year.[k]	Bill, joint resolution, amendment, motion, or conference report.	Simple majority
425(a)(1)	Prohibits consideration of legislation reported by a committee unless the committee has published a statement by CBO on the direct costs of federal mandates.	Bill or joint resolution.	Simple majoritye
425(a)(2)	Prohibits consideration of legislation that would increase the direct costs of federal intergovernmental mandates by an amount greater than the thresholds specified in Section 424(a).	Bill, joint resolution, amendment, motion, or conference report.	Simple majoritye

Table 1 (Continued)

Section	Description	Application	Senate Waiver Votea
426	In the House, prohibits consideration of a rule or order that would waive the application of Section 425.	Resolution, rule, or order.	n/a

Source: The Congressional Budget Act of 1974 (P.L. 93-344), as amended. U.S. Congress. House Committee on the Budget, Compilation of Laws and Rules Relating to the Congressional Budget Process, 1 10th Congress, 2nd session, November 2008 (Washington: GPO, 2008), pp. 3-60.

[a] This column indicates the type of Senate vote (as provided under Section 904 of the Congressional Budget Act) necessary to approve a motion to waive the point of order listed. The term "simple majority" means that the provision may be waived by a majority vote of the Members voting, a quorum being present. The term "three-fifths" means that a motion to waive the provision must be approved by three-fifths of the Members "duly chosen and sworn." For those provisions, which are marked with an asterisk (*), the three-fifths requirement is scheduled to expire on September 30, 2017, (as identified under Section 904(e) and extended under S.Con.Res. 21 (110th Congress)), reverting to simple majority after that time. See footnote 7 in the text of this chapter for details on previous extensions. The same voting requirement (either simple majority or three-fifths) would also apply to a vote to appeal a ruling of the chair connected with a point of order. The term "n/a" is used for those provisions that apply in the House only.

[b] Section 302(g) of the Congressional Budget Act (known as the Pay-As-You-Go exception) provides that Sections 302(f)(1), 303(a) (after April 15), and 311(a), as it applies to revenues, shall not apply in the House to legislation (bill, joint resolution, amendment, or conference report) if for each fiscal year covered by the most recently agreed to budget resolution such legislation would not increase the deficit if added to other changes in revenues or direct spending provided in the budget resolution pursuant to pay-as-you-go procedures included under Section 301 (b)(8).

[c] In the 109th Congress, the House adopted a provision in H.Res. 248 establishing that during the 109th Congress there would be a separate point of order in the Committee of the Whole against a motion to rise and report a general appropriations bill if that bill, as amended, were in a breach of the appropriate 302(b) allocation. This provision was subsequently readopted in the 110th and 111th Congresses as a separate order of the House (see Section 3(a)(4) of H.Res. 5 (111th Congress)).

[d] Section 303(b) sets forth exceptions to the prohibitions under 303(a). In the House, the point of order does not apply to (1) advance discretionary new budget authority that first become available for the first or second fiscal year after the first fiscal year covered in a

budget resolution; (2) revenue legislation that is to first become effective after the first fiscal year covered in a budget resolution; (3) general appropriations bills after May 15; or (4) any bill or joint resolution unless it is reported by a committee (see also table note b above for an additional exception to 303(a) provided under Section 302(g)). In the Senate, the point of order does not apply to advance appropriations for the first or second fiscal year after the first fiscal year covered in a budget resolution. The application of this point of order to appropriations bills in the Senate is provided specifically under Section 303(c), which requires an allocation be made to the Senate Appropriations Committee under Section 302(a) as well as agreement on a budget resolution.

[e] The points of order under Sections 303(a), 303(c), 425(a), and 425(b) were made subject to the three-fifths threshold under Section 403(b) of H.Con.Res. 95 (109th Congress). Section 205 of S.Con.Res. 21 (110th Congress) provides that Section 403 of H.Con.Res. 95 (109th Congress) shall no longer apply in the Senate.

[f] Section 204(g) of H.Con.Res. 290 (106th Congress) provided that for purposes of interpreting Section 305(b)(2) of the Budget Act, an amendment not be considered germane if it contains predominately precatory language (e.g., Sense of the Senate provisions), although this addition may not be enforceable.

[g] By standing order of the House, the application of this section to resolutions is construed in the House as a reference to a joint resolution (see Section 3(a)(1) of H.Res. 5 (111th Congress)).

[h] In the House, the impact of amendments is measured in relation to the levels in the reconciliation measure. In the Senate, the impact is measured in relation to the levels provided in the reconciliation instructions which relate to the measure.

[i] Section 311(c) provides that 311(a) shall not apply in the House to legislation that would not cause a committee's spending allocation under 302(a) to be exceeded.

[j] Section 251(c) of the Balanced Budget and Emergency Deficit Control Act of 1985, as amended, expired at the end of FY2002.

[k] Currently no maximum deficit amounts are specified under the Balanced Budget and Emergency Deficit Control Act of 1985, as amended.

[l] For more information on this provision (known as the "Byrd Rule"), see CRS Report RL30862, The Budget Reconciliation Process: The Senate's "Byrd Rule", by Bill Heniff Jr.

[m] Section 401(d) provides that Sections 401(a) and 401(b) shall not apply to new spending authority described in those sections that flow from (1) a trust fund established under the Social Security Act or any other trust fund for which 90% or more of its expenditures are supported by dedicated revenues; (2) certain wholly owned or mixed ownership government corporations; or (3) gifts or bequests made to the United States for a specific purpose.

Table 2. Points of Order Under S.Con.Res. 13 (1 1 1 th Congress) (Budget Resolution for FY20 10)

Section	Description	Application	Senate Waiver Votea
401(a)	In the Senate, prohibits the consideration of a measure or provisions that would exceed any of the discretionary limits for FY2009-FY2010 specified in Section 401(b), including any adjustments made under the provisions of Section 401(c).	Bill, joint resolution, amendment, motion, or conference report.	Three-fifths
402(a)	In the Senate, prohibits the consideration of advance appropriations, except as specified in this budget resolution.[b]	Bill, joint resolution, amendment, motion, or conference report.	Three-fifths
403(e)	In the Senate, provides for a point of order against the use of an emergency designation as allowed under Section 403(a) of this budget resolution to provide for exemption in the Senate from budget enforcement mechanisms specified in Section 403(b).[c]	Bill, resolution, amendment, motion, or conference report	Three-fifths
404(a)	In the Senate, prohibits the consideration of direct spending or revenue legislation that would cause a net increase in the deficit in excess of $10 billion in any fiscal year provided for in the most recently adopted budget resolution unless it is fully offset over the period of all fiscal years provided for in the most recently adopted budget resolution.[d]	Bill, joint resolution, amendment, motion, or conference report.	Three-fifths
405(a)	In the Senate, prohibits consideration of any measure or provision that extends or reauthorizes surface transportation programs that appropriates budget authority from sources other than the Highway Trust Fund.d	Bill, joint resolution, amendment, or conference report	Three-fifths
424(a)	In the House, prohibits the consideration of advance appropriations, except as provided in this budget resolution.[e]	Bill, joint resolution, amendment, or conference report.	n/a

Source: S.Con.Res. 13 (111th Congress).

[a] This column indicates the type of Senate vote necessary to approve a motion to waive the point of order listed. The term "three-fifths" means that a motion to waive the provision must be approved by three-fifths of the Members "duly chosen and sworn." The same voting requirement would also apply to a vote to appeal a ruling of the chair connected with the point of order.

[b] This section limits consideration in the Senate of advance appropriations, except that advance appropriations may be provided for FY20 11 -FY20 12 for accounts specified in the joint explanatory statement of the conference report for this budget resolution (H.Rept. 111-89) in an aggregate amount not to exceed $28.852 billion in each year. See also the point of order in the House under Section 424 of this budget resolution.

[c] This section concerns the use of emergency designations, but does not establish a point of order against the spending or revenue itself. It also requires committees reporting legislation that include provisions designated as emergency to include in any accompanying written report a justification for the designation. The use of an emergency designation exempts resulting new budget authority, outlays or receipts for purposes of enforcing Sections 302 and 311 of the Budget Act, Sections 401 and 404 of this budget resolution, Section 311 of S.Con.Res. 70 (110th Congress) (see Table 3), and Section 201 of S.Con.Res. 21 (110th Congress) (see Table 4). This point of order supersedes earlier, similar points of order under H.Con.Res. 68 and H.Con.Res. 290 (both 106th Congress), H.Con.Res. 95 (108th Congress), Section 1 4007(b)(2) of P.L. 108-287, H.Con.Res. 95 (109th Congress), and S.Con.Res. 21 (110th Congress). No expiration date is provided for the current point of order. Note that while there is no similar point of order in the House, Section 423 of this budget resolution provides that appropriations for discretionary amounts designated as necessary to meet emergency needs shall not count for purposes of the Budget Act or this budget resolution.

[d] This section is scheduled to expire on September 30, 2018.

[e] This section limits the consideration in the House of advance appropriations, except that advance appropriations may be provided for FY20 11 -FY20 12 for those accounts specified in the joint explanatory statement of the conference report for this budget resolution H.Rept. 111-89 in an aggregate amount not to exceed $28.852 billion. See also the point of order in the Senate as provided in Section 402 of this budget resolution.

Table 3. Points of Order Under S.Con.Res. 70 (1 10th Congress) (Budget Resolution for FY2009)

Section	Description	Application	Senate Waiver Vote[a]
311(b)	In the Senate, prohibits the consideration of a measure that would cause a net increase in deficits in excess of $5 billion in any of the four 10-year periods beginning in 2019 through 2058.[b]	Bill, joint resolution, amendment, motion, or conference report.	Three-fifths
314(a)	In the Senate, prohibits the consideration of appropriations legislation that includes a change in a mandatory program producing net costs as defined in Section 314(b).[c]	Appropriations measure, amendment, motion, or conference report.	Three-fifths

Source: S.Con.Res. 70 (1 10th Congress).

a This column indicates the type of Senate vote necessary to approve a motion to waive the point of order listed. The term "three-fifths" means that a motion to waive the provision must be approved by three-fifths of the Members "duly chosen and sworn." The same voting requirement would also apply to a vote to appeal a ruling of the chair connected with the point of order.

b This point of order supersedes earlier, similar points of order provided in H.Con.Res. 95 (108th Congress) and S.Con.Res. 21 (110th Congress). This section is scheduled to expire on September 30, 2017.

c This point of order supersedes an earlier, similar point of order provided in S.Con.Res. 21 (110th Congress).

Table 4. Points of Order Under S.Con.Res. 21 (1 10th Congress) (Budget Resolution for FY2008)

Section	Description	Application	Senate Waiver Vote[a]
201(a)	In the Senate, prohibits consideration of any direct spending or revenue legislation that would increase or cause an on-budget deficit for the period of the current fiscal year and the five ensuing fiscal years or the period of the current fiscal year and the ten ensuing fiscal years.[b]	Bill, joint resolution, amendment, or conference report.	Three-fifths
202(a)	In the Senate, prohibits consideration of reconciliation legislation that would increase or cause a deficit (or decrease a surplus) for the period of the current fiscal year and the five ensuing fiscal years or the period of the current fiscal year and the ten ensuing fiscal years.	Bill, resolution, amendment, amendment between the houses, or conference report.	Three-fifths

Source: S.Con.Res. 21 (1 10th Congress)

[a] This column indicates the type of Senate vote necessary to approve a motion to waive the point of order listed. The term "three-fifths" means that a motion to waive the provision must be approved by three-fifths of the Members "duly chosen and sworn." The same voting requirement would also apply to a vote to appeal a ruling of the chair connected with the point of order.

[b] This point of order supersedes earlier, similar points of order provided in H.Con.Res. 67 (104th Congress), H.Con.Res. 68 (106th Congress), and H.Con.Res. 95 (108th Congress). This section is scheduled to expire on September 30, 2017. Paragraph 5 of this section specifically excludes the budget resolution or legislation that affects or continues the full funding of the deposit insurance guarantee commitment in effect on the date of enactment of the Budget Enforcement Act of 1990. Paragraph 6 of this section provides that the point of order would not apply in cases in which direct spending and revenue legislation when taken together with other direct spending and revenue legislation enacted since the beginning of the calendar year (and not accounted for in the baseline) result in a net decrease in the deficit (or increase in the surplus), although deficit reduction legislation enacted pursuant to reconciliation instructions may not be used in such calculations.

Table 5. Points of Order Under the Standing Rules of the House (1 1 1 th Congress) (as adopted under H.Res. 5, 111th Congress)

Rule and clause	Description	Application
XXI, clause 7	In the House, prohibits consideration of a budget resolution that includes reconciliation instructions that would provide for an increase in the deficit (or decrease in the surplus) for the period comprising the current fiscal year, the budget year, and the four fiscal years following that budget year, or the current fiscal year, the budget year, and the nine fiscal years following that budget year.[a]	Budget resolution, amendment, or conference report.
XXI, clause 10	In the House, prohibits consideration of any direct spending or revenue legislation that would have the net effect of increasing the deficit (or reducing the surplus) for the period comprising the current fiscal year, the budget year, and the four fiscal years following that budget year, or the current fiscal year, the budget year, and the nine fiscal years following that budget year.[b]	Bill, joint resolution, amendment, or conference report.

Source: H.Res. 5 (111th Congress), H.Res. 1500 (111th Congress).

[a] This point of order supersedes an earlier, similar point of order first adopted by the House as part of the rules of the House for the 110th Congress.

[b] Rule XXI, clause 10(b) provides that when a measure is considered by the House under the terms of a special order directing the Clerk to add at the end of the measure, the provisions of another measure previously passed by the House, those additional provisions are included in determining the application of this point of order. This point of order supersedes an earlier, similar point of order first adopted as part of the rules of the House for the 110th Congress. The rule was modified in Section 5 of H.Res. 1500 (111th Congress) to align with the Statutory Pay-As-You-Go Act of 2010 (P.L. 111-139), including a change to the time periods and the exclusion of the budgetary effects resulting from extending current policy in four specified policy areas. For more on the House Pay-As-You-Go rule see CRS Report R4 1510, Budget Enforcement Procedures: House Pay-As-You-Go (PAYGO) Rule, by Bill Heniff Jr.

Table 6. Point of Order Under P.L. 1 01-508 (Budget Enforcement Act of 1990)

Section	Description	Application
13302(a)	In the House, prohibits consideration of legislation that would provide for a net increase in Social Security benefits or decrease in Social Security taxes in excess of 0.02% of the present value of future taxable payroll for a 75-year period, or in excess of $250,000,000 for the first five-year period after it becomes effective.a	Bill, joint resolution, amendment, or conference report.

Source: Subtitle C of the Budget Enforcement Act of 1990 (Title XIII of the Omnibus Budget Reconciliation Act of 1990).

[a]. Section 13302(b) provides that the point of order would not apply to legislation that reduces Social Security taxes in excess of the threshold amounts if these reductions are offset by equivalent increases in Medicare taxes.

Table 7. Point of Order Under P.L. 111-139 (Statutory Pay-As-You-Go Act of 2010)

Section	Description	Application	Senate Waiver Vote[a]
4(g)(3)	In the Senate, if a point of order is raised during consideration of legislation subject to PAYGO against an emergency designation in that measure, the provision making the designation shall be stricken.[b]	Bill, joint resolution, amendment, or conference report.	Three-fifths

Source: P.L. 111-139.

[a] This column indicates the type of Senate vote necessary to approve a motion to waive the point of order listed. The term "three-fifths" means that a motion to waive the provision must be approved by three-fifths of the Members "duly chosen and sworn." The same voting requirement would also apply to a vote to appeal a ruling of the chair connected with the point of order.

[b] For more information on the Statutory Pa-As-You-Go Act of 2010 see CRS Report R41157, The Statutory Pay-As-You-Go Act of 2010: Summary and Legislative History, by Bill Heniff Jr.

PROCEDURES FOR WAIVING POINTS OF ORDER

The Congressional Budget Act sets forth certain procedures, under Section 904, for waiving points of order under the act. These waiver procedures apply in the Senate only. Under these procedures, a Senator may make a motion to waive the application of a point of order either preemptively before it can be raised, or after it is raised, but before the presiding officer rules on its merits.[6]

In the Senate, most points of order under the Budget Act may be waived by a vote of at least three-fifths of all Senators duly chosen and sworn (60 votes if there are no vacancies) (see **Table 1**). The three-fifths waiver requirement was first established for some points of order under the Balanced Budget and Emergency Deficit Control Act of 1985. Beginning with the Balanced Budget Act of 1997, this super-majority threshold was applied to several additional points of order on a temporary basis. These points of order are identified in Section 904(c)(2), and the three-fifths requirement is currently scheduled to expire September 30, 2017.[7] The three-fifths threshold has also been required for the Senate to waive the application of many of the points of order established in recent budget resolutions, such as the PAYGO point of order. As with other provisions of Senate rules, Budget Act points of order also may be waived by unanimous consent.

In the House, Budget Act points of order are typically waived by the adoption of special rules, although other means (such as unanimous consent or suspension of the rules) may also be used. A waiver may be used to protect a bill, specified provision(s) in a bill, or an amendment from a point of order that could be raised against it. Waivers may be granted for one or more amendments even if they are not granted for the underlying bill. The House may waive the application of one or more specific points of order, or they may include a "blanket waiver," that is, a waiver that would protect a bill, provision, or amendment from any point of order.

End Notes

1 The Congressional Budget Act (Titles I-IX of P.L. 93-344) has been amended on a number of occasions since its enactment. The most salient of the modifications has been as a result of the Balanced Budget and Emergency Deficit Control Act of 1985 (P.L. 99-177, also known as Gramm-Rudman-Hollings or GRH); the Balanced Budget and Emergency Deficit Control Reaffirmation Act of 1987 (P.L. 100-119); the Budget Enforcement Act of 1990 (Title XIII of the Omnibus Budget Reconciliation Act of 1990, P.L. 101-508); Title XIV of the Omnibus Budget Reconciliation Act of 1993 (P.L. 103-66); and Title X of the Balanced Budget Act of 1997 (P.L. 105-33). For the text of the Budget Act, as amended, see U.S. Congress, House Committee on the Budget, *Compilation of Laws and Rules Relating to the*

Congressional Budget Process, 1 10th Cong., 2nd sess., November 2008 (Washington: GPO, 2008), pp. 3-60.

[2] The reconciliation process is an optional procedure set forth in Section 310 of the Congressional Budget Act. First used in 1980, reconciliation is a two-step process triggered when the budget resolution includes instructions to one or more committee(s) directing them to recommend changes in revenue or spending laws necessary to achieve the overall levels agreed to. The recommendations are then considered in one or more reconciliation measures under expedited procedures. Certain features of the reconciliation process are enforced by points of order that are included in this chapter. For more on the reconciliation process generally, see CRS Report RL33030, *The Budget Reconciliation Process: House and Senate Procedures*, by Robert Keith and Bill Heniff Jr.

[3] For example, the prohibition against motions to recommit concurrent resolutions on the budget in the House under Section 305(a)(2) of the act is typically not counted as a separate point of order. Likewise, the requirement under Section 308(a) of the act for reports on legislation to include cost estimates is not formulated as a point of order, although the House has deemed it necessary to formally waive the provision on occasion.

[4] The expiration of the provisions of the Balanced Budget and Emergency Deficit Control Act at the end of FY2002 has rendered moot a number of points of order. For example, points of order provided in the Congressional Budget Act to allow the Senate to enforce discretionary spending limits (Section 3 12(b)) or maximum deficit amounts (Section 312(c)) have been rendered moot because no statute currently specifies such a limit or amount.

[5] Section 313(d) provides a special procedure for further consideration of a measure should a point of order under this section be sustained against a provision in a conference report.

[6] In the case of points of order under Section 313 of the Budget Act (and by extension, points of order under Sections 402 and 403 of S.Con.Res. 13 (11 1th Congress)), as well as points of order under Section 314 of S.Con.Res. 70 (1 10th Congress), a single point of order may be raised against several provisions. The Presiding Officer may sustain the point of order "as to some or all of the provisions," and a motion to waive the point of order may, likewise, be made concerning some or all of the provisions against which the point of order was raised.

[7] As originally provided in Title X of the Balanced Budget Act of 1997, the three-fifths requirement expired on September 30, 2002. The Senate subsequently adopted S.Res. 304 on October 16, 2002, renewing the three-fifths requirement for all of the points of order identified in Section 904(c)(2) (except for Section 302(f)(2)(B)) through April 15, 2003. The three-fifths requirement (including for Section 302(f)(2)(B)) was renewed through September 30, 2008, under Section 503 of H.Con.Res. 95 (108th Congress), extended through September 30, 2010, under Section 403 of H.Con.Res. 95 (109th Congress), and is currently extended through September 30, 2017, under Section 205 of S.Con.Res. 21 (110th Congress).

In: United States Federal Budget Process
Editors: Gerard T. Brenner et al.
ISBN: 978-1-61209-844-9

Chapter 3

BASELINES AND SCOREKEEPING IN THE FEDERAL BUDGET PROCESS

Bill Heniff, Jr.

INTRODUCTION

Baselines and scorekeeping are an integral part of the federal budget process, providing lawmakers with a framework for making and enforcing budgetary decisions. The existing-law baseline, currently used by Congress, is a projection of federal spending, revenue, and the deficit (or surplus) that would occur if existing law were left unchanged. The baseline serves as a benchmark for federal budget decisions. Scorekeeping is the process by which the budgetary impact of proposed and enacted budget policies is measured; it assists Congress in making and enforcing budgetary decisions. This chapter provides a brief explanation of baselines and scorekeeping and their uses in the federal budget process.

BASELINES

A baseline is an estimate of federal spending and receipts during a fiscal year under existing law. Congress set forth in law specific rules for calculating the direct spending, receipts, and discretionary spending baselines in Section

257 of the Balanced Budget and Emergency Deficit Control Act of 1985 (Title II of P.L. 99-177), as amended. Direct spending and receipts are assumed to continue at the level prescribed by existing law. These projections are based upon economic assumptions (e.g., economic growth, inflation, and unemployment) and other technical assumptions (e.g., demographic and workload changes) about future years. Discretionary spending is assumed to continue at the level of the current year's spending level adjusted "sequentially and cumulatively" for inflation and other factors.

A baseline provides a benchmark for comparing proposed budget policy changes to existing policies and indicating changes that may be necessary to meet certain budget policy goals. Therefore, the calculation of a baseline can be instrumental to the evaluation of budget policies. Two baselines are commonly cited in the federal budget process: the *current services estimates* calculated by the Office of Management and Budget (OMB) and the *budget baseline projections* calculated by the Congressional Budget Office (CBO). Each generally follows the rules set forth in Section 257 of the Deficit Control Act of 1985, as described above.[1] However, OMB and CBO make their own economic and technical assumptions, reflecting different projections about future economic and program performance. Thus, the estimated levels of spending and revenues may differ between the current services estimates and the budget baseline projections.

SCOREKEEPING

Scorekeeping is the process of measuring the budgetary effects of pending and enacted legislation against the baseline. The process allows Congress to compare proposed budget policy changes to existing law and to enforce budget constraints, such as the spending and revenue levels agreed upon in the budget resolution and the congressional and statutory pay-as-you-go (PAYGO) requirements.

In the congressional budget process, scorekeeping is the responsibility of the House and Senate Budget Committees, acting with the assistance of CBO. Section 308(b) of the 1974 Congressional Budget Act requires the Budget Committees to make available, to their respective chambers, monthly summary scorekeeping reports on the current status of congressional budget actions. Section 308(a) of the Budget Act requires that any measure reported by a committee include estimates of the budgetary impact of the proposed legislation. These estimates, usually in the form of a statement in the accompanying committee report or published separately in the *Congressional Record*, are calculated by CBO. For revenue measures, CBO is required to rely on estimates provided by the Joint Committee on Taxation (Section 201(f) of the Budget Act).

Generally, scorekeeping is used to determine whether proposed legislation violates the budget resolution levels and other budget rules, such as the House and Senate PAYGO rules. Under the Budget Act, for example, any measure that violates the aggregate spending and revenue levels of the most recently passed budget resolution or the subsequent committee allocation levels generally is subject to a point of order.[2] Section 312 of the Budget Act requires that the determination of such violations, and any other enforcement provisions in the Budget Act, be based on estimates made by the House and Senate Budget Committees. Similarly, the House and Senate PAYGO rules (House Rule XXI, clause 10, and Section 201 of S.Con.Res. 21, the FY2008 budget resolution, respectively) require that a determination on whether direct spending or revenue legislation increases the deficit must be based on estimates made by the House and Senate Budget Committees.[3]

For statutory PAYGO purposes, the Statutory PAYGO Act (Title I of P.L. 111-139, 124 Stat. 8-29) provides that OMB is responsible for maintaining five- and 10-year PAYGO scorecards to record the budgetary effects of enacted legislation on the deficit.[4] It also provides that the budgetary effects of individual direct spending and revenue legislation are to be determined either by a reference in the legislation to a statement of budgetary effects submitted for printing in the *Congressional Record* by the chair of the House or Senate Budget Committee prior to passage, or by OMB if no appropriate reference in the legislation or statement exists.[5]

To minimize any scorekeeping differences between the House and Senate Budget Committees, OMB, and CBO, some of the key scorekeeping guidelines currently in use were set forth in the joint explanatory statement accompanying the conference report to the Balanced Budget Act of 1997 (H.Rept. 105-2 17, pp. 1007-10 14). These guidelines generally reflect the standard scorekeeping practices used since the Budget Enforcement Act of 1990 (Title XIII of P.L. 101- 508). The scorekeeping guidelines are reviewed periodically. Any changes to these guidelines must be agreed to by the House and Senate Budget Committees, OMB, and CBO.

End Notes

[1] Until the expiration of this section at the end of FY2006, CBO was required to follow the provisions of Section 257 in producing its baseline projections. CBO has indicated that it would follow these practices until directed otherwise by Congress. See, for example, CBO, *The Budget and Economic Outlook: Fiscal Years 2008 to 2017*, p. xi, fn. 1.

[2] For additional information on points of order under the Budget Act and their application, see CRS Report 97-865, *Points of Order in the Congressional Budget Process*, by James V. Saturno.

[3] For additional information on the House and Senate PAYGO rules, see CRS Report R41510, *Budget Enforcement Procedures: House Pay-As-You-Go (PAYGO) Rule*, by Bill Heniff Jr., and CRS Report RL3 1943, *Budget Enforcement Procedures: Senate Pay-As-You-Go (PAYGO) Rule*, by Bill Heniff Jr.

[4] While the Statutory PAYGO Act requires the placement of the budgetary effects of legislation on five-year and 10- year scorecards, it also requires that any budgetary effects in the current year shall be treated as though they occurred in the budget year (i.e., the first year of the five- and 10-year periods), effectively applying the PAYGO requirement over six-year and 11-year periods.

[5] For additional information on the Statutory PAYGO Act, see CRS Report R41 157, *The Statutory Pay-As-You-Go Act of 2010: Summary and Legislative History*, by Bill Heniff Jr.

In: United States Federal Budget Process ISBN: 978-1-61209-844-9
Editors: Gerard T. Brenner et al.

Chapter 4

ALLOCATIONS AND SUBDIVISIONS IN THE CONGRESSIONAL BUDGET PROCESS

Bill Heniff, Jr.

The annual budget resolution sets forth total spending and revenue levels for at least five fiscal years. The spending amounts are allocated, or "crosswalked," to the House and Senate committees having jurisdiction over discretionary spending (the Appropriations Committees) and direct spending (the legislative committees). The committee allocations provide Congress with one means of enforcing the spending levels of a budget resolution after it has been adopted.

While the budget resolution allocates spending among the 20 major functional categories of the federal budget for the purpose of providing a broad statement of budget priorities, the functional categories do not correspond to the committee system by which Congress operates. The committee allocations reformulate the functional category amounts in a budget resolution to correspond to committee jurisdictions. By allocating the spending among committees responsible for spending legislation, the committee allocations allow Congress to hold its committees accountable for staying within the spending limits established in the budget resolution.

Section 302(a) of the Congressional Budget Act of 1974 (Titles I-IX of P.L. 93-344, 88 Stat. 297- 332), as amended, requires that the total budget authority and outlays set forth in the budget resolution be allocated to each House and Senate committee that has jurisdiction over specific spending legislation. These committee allocations usually are included in the joint explanatory statement accompanying the conference report on a budget resolution. Section 302(b) of the Budget Act requires the Appropriations Committee of each chamber to subdivide its committee allocation among its subcommittees as soon as practicable after a budget resolution has been adopted. The Appropriations Committees are then required to report these subdivisions to their respective chamber and may revise the subdivisions any time during the appropriations process to reflect actions taken on spending legislation. Section 3 02(c) of the Budget Act provides a point of order against the consideration of any appropriations measures before the Appropriations Committees report their subdivisions.

The spending allocations may be revised after a budget resolution has been adopted if provided for in the resolution. For instance, Congress usually includes reserve fund provisions in the annual budget resolution, which provide the chairs of the House and Senate Budget Committees the authority to revise the committee spending allocations if certain legislation is reported by the appropriate committee or other conditions are met.

The House and Senate Appropriations Committees have jurisdiction over the regular appropriations acts and other appropriations acts. The Appropriations Committees of each chamber have parallel subcommittees, each of which is responsible for one of the regular appropriations acts. After extensive hearings, each of the subcommittees reports one of the regular appropriations bills to its respective full committee. Then, the full Appropriations Committees report the bills to their respective chamber. A cost estimate of each bill is prepared and compared to the amount allocated or subdivided to the relevant subcommittee.

Section 302(f) of the Budget Act prohibits any measure or amendment that would cause the 302(a) or 302(b) allocations to be exceeded. In the House, these committee allocations and suballocations are the primary focus of enforcement since Section 311(c) of the Budget Act, known as the "Fazio exception," allows the overall limit of spending to be breached so long as a committee's 302(a) allocation is not exceeded.

The allocation limits are not self-enforcing; a Member must raise a point of order for an allocation to be enforced. The points of order may also be waived. In the House, a special rule may be adopted, or unanimous consent may be granted, waiving any budgetary points of order. In the Senate, the point of order against violations of the spending allocations may be waived by a motion under Section 904 of the Budget Act or by unanimous consent. A motion to waive the point of order requires a three-fifths vote of all Senators duly sworn and chosen (60 votes if there is no more than one vacancy).

In: United States Federal Budget Process
Editors: Gerard T. Brenner et al.
ISBN: 978-1-61209-844-9

Chapter 5

ENTITLEMENTS AND APPROPRIATED ENTITLEMENTS IN THE FEDERAL BUDGET PROCESS

Bill Heniff, Jr.

Entitlements are programs that require payments to persons, state or local governments, or other entities if specific eligibility criteria established in the authorizing law are met. Entitlement payments are legal obligations of the federal government, and eligible beneficiaries may have legal recourse if full payment under the law is not provided. This chapter provides a brief explanation of spending for entitlements, including so-called appropriated entitlements, and discusses the procedural and statutory constraints on legislation affecting such entitlement spending.

ENTITLEMENT SPENDING

Entitlement spending is a form of mandatory spending (also referred to as direct spending), which currently comprises more than half of total federal spending. Spending on entitlements is not controlled through the annual appropriations process. Instead, entitlement spending is based on the eligibility and benefit criteria established in law, which is under the jurisdiction of the various authorizing committees of the House and Senate. The total amount of spending on entitlements is determined by the aggregate total of all individual benefits. Most entitlement spending, such as for Medicare, is not capped at a specific spending level, and typically increases (but may decrease) each year as the number of eligible beneficiaries and the authorized benefit payments increases (or decreases). However, some entitlement spending—particularly entitlement payments to states, such as the State Children's Health Insurance Program (commonly referred to as CHIP)—is capped at a specific level provided in the authorizing law.

Most entitlement spending bypasses the annual appropriations process altogether and is funded by permanent or multi-year appropriations in substantive law. Such spending becomes available automatically each year, without legislative action by Congress. Examples of such programs include Social Security, Medicare, and federal employee retirement.

A portion of entitlement spending, such as Medicaid and certain veterans' programs, is funded in annual appropriations acts. Such entitlement spending, referred to as *appropriated entitlements*, comprises roughly 36%-38% of funding provided in the annual appropriations acts. While the funding is provided in the annual appropriations acts, the level of spending for appropriated entitlements is not controlled through the annual appropriations process. Instead, the level of spending for appropriated entitlements, like other entitlements, is based on the benefit and eligibility criteria established in law, and the amount provided in appropriations acts is based on meeting this projected level.

PROCEDURAL CONTROLS ON ENTITLEMENT SPENDING LEGISLATION

The Congressional Budget Act of 1974 (Titles I-IX of P.L. 93-344, 2 U.S.C. 60 1-688), as amended, provides for the annual adoption of a budget resolution to serve as a framework for the consideration of budgetary legislation each year. Accordingly, the budget resolution contains projected spending levels, including entitlement spending, under existing law, adjusted for any proposed policy changes, for a period of at least five fiscal years. The projected spending totals, however, do not include spending for the largest entitlement program, Social Security, which is excluded by law from the totals and presented separately.

The budget resolution also may include reconciliation directives instructing House and Senate authorizing committees to recommend legislative changes to existing laws affecting entitlements to meet the recommended levels of spending. Once reported, such reconciliation legislation is considered under special procedures on the House and Senate floor.[1]

Separate from any reconciliation directives, entitlement spending legislation may originate under the normal legislative process, initiated by the authorizing committees or individual members. Section 303 of the Budget Act, however, prohibits entitlement spending legislation from being considered before a budget resolution has been adopted.

When entitlement spending legislation is considered, its content is restricted under the rules of the congressional budget process. First, Section 302(f) of the Budget Act prohibits the consideration of any entitlement legislation that would cause a committee to exceed its spending allocation associated with the most recently adopted budget resolution for the first fiscal year or the total of all fiscal years. A committee's spending allocation, commonly referred to as its Section 302(a) spending allocation, reflects the amount of mandatory spending, including entitlement spending, under its jurisdiction. Second, Section 311 of the Budget Act prohibits consideration of any entitlement legislation that would cause spending to exceed the agreed upon total spending levels contained in the budget resolution for the first fiscal year.[2] Third, Section 401(b) of the Budget Act generally prohibits the consideration of any legislation providing new entitlement spending that would become effective in the current fiscal year.

In addition, both the House and Senate have "pay-as-you-go" (PAYGO) requirements for entitlement spending legislation. The House and Senate PAYGO rules (Rule XXI, clause 10, and Section 201 of S.Con.Res. 21, the FY2008 budget resolution, respectively) generally prohibit the consideration of legislation affecting entitlement spending (as well as revenues) that would have the net effect of increasing the deficit (or in the House, reducing the surplus) over either a six- year period covering the current fiscal year plus the ensuing five fiscal years or an 11-year period covering the current fiscal year plus the ensuing 10 fiscal years.[3]

Finally, legislation affecting the Social Security program, the largest entitlement, also is constrained by congressional budget procedures. First, a budget resolution that would decrease the Social Security surplus is subject to a point of order in the Senate under Section 301(i) of the Budget Act. Second, Section 31 1(a)(3) provides a point of order in the Senate against any legislation that would cause Social Security surpluses to decrease or deficits to increase relative to the levels set forth in a budget resolution. In addition, Section 13302 of the Budget Enforcement Act of 1990 (Title XIII of P.L. 101-508) established a point of order in the House prohibiting the consideration of any legislation that would change certain balances of the Social Security trust funds over specified periods. Lastly, a point of order under Section 310(g) may be raised in the House and Senate against a reconciliation bill that contains recommendations relating to the Social Security program.

A point of order is the procedural mechanism for enforcing the rules governing the consideration of entitlement spending legislation. Points of order, however, are not self-enforcing: a Member must raise a point of order to enforce such rules. Budget enforcement points of order also may be waived. In the House, a point of order may be waived by unanimous consent, by suspension of the rules, or by a special rule reported by the Rules Committee and adopted by the full House. In the Senate, points of order under the Budget Act or provided in budget resolutions, such as the PAYGO point of order, may be waived by unanimous consent or by motion as provided under Section 904 of the Budget Act. A motion to waive most Budget Act points of order requires an affirmative vote of three-fifths of all Senators duly chosen and sworn (60 votes if there are no vacancies); Section 303 of the Budget Act may be waived by a majority vote.

Statutory Controls on Entitlement Spending Legislation

Entitlement spending legislation is also controlled by the Statutory Pay-As-You-Go Act of 2010 (Title I of P.L. 111-139, 124 Stat. 8-29). Like the House and Senate PAYGO rules, the statutory PAYGO rule is intended to discourage or prevent Congress from taking certain legislative action that would increase the on-budget deficit.[4] It generally requires that legislation affecting entitlement spending (and revenues) not increase the deficit over a six-year and 11-year period.[5]

The statutory PAYGO requirement is enforced by sequestration—the cancellation of budgetary resources provided by laws affecting direct spending—to eliminate an increase in the deficit resulting from the enactment of legislation. Generally, the statutory PAYGO rule provides that if the net effect of new entitlement spending and revenue legislation enacted during a year increases the deficit (i.e., violates the PAYGO requirement), budgetary resources in certain entitlement spending programs are cut in order to eliminate the increase in the deficit.

Many entitlement spending programs and activities, including Social Security benefits, veterans' programs, retirement and disability benefits, and low-income programs, among others, are exempt from any sequestration. In addition, the amount of any sequestration is limited to 4% for Medicare and 2% for certain health and medical care activities.

End Notes

[1] For further information on the reconciliation process, see CRS Report RL33030, *The Budget Reconciliation Process: House and Senate Procedures*, by Robert Keith and Bill Heniff Jr.

[2] For further information on the enforcement of the budget resolution, see CRS Report 98-8 15, *Budget Resolution Enforcement*, by Bill Heniff Jr.

[3] For further information on these PAYGO rules, see CRS Report R41510, *Budget Enforcement Procedures: House Pay-As-You-Go (PAYGO) Rule*, by Bill Heniff Jr., and CRS Report RL3 1943, *Budget Enforcement Procedures: Senate Pay-As-You-Go (PAYGO) Rule*, by Bill Heniff Jr.

[4] For more detailed information on the statutory requirement, see CRS Report R41 157, *The Statutory Pay-As-You-Go Act of 2010: Summary and Legislative History*, by Bill Heniff Jr.

[5] The PAYGO statute exempts certain direct spending and revenue provisions from being counted for purposes of the PAYGO requirement: (1) provisions designated as an emergency; and (2) provisions extending current policy in four specified areas, which are scheduled by statute to expire, within certain constraints. One of the four current policy areas affects entitlement spending: Medicare payments to physicians. The other current policy areas affect revenues: (1) estate and gift tax; (2) alternative minimum tax (AMT); and (3) middle-class tax cuts.

In: United States Federal Budget Process ISBN: 978-1-61209-844-9
Editors: Gerard T. Brenner, et al.

Chapter 6

BASIC FEDERAL BUDGETING TERMINOLOGY

Bill Heniff, Jr.

In its most elemental form, the federal budget is a comprehensive accounting of the government's spending, revenues, and borrowing. This chapter provides a brief overview of the basic terminology and concepts used in the federal budget process.

FISCAL YEAR

The *fiscal year* is the accounting period of the federal government. It begins on October 1 and ends on September 30 of the next calendar year. Each fiscal year is identified by the calendar year in which it ends and commonly is referred to as "FY." For example, FY20 11 began October 1, 2010, and ends September 30, 2011.

SPENDING

The key terms of federal spending are *budget authority, obligations, outlays,* and *spendout rate*. Congress and the President enact budget authority in law. Budget authority allows federal agencies to incur obligations, such as entering into contracts, employing personnel, and submitting purchase orders. Outlays represent the actual payment of these obligations, usually in the form of electronic transfers or checks issued by the Treasury Department. The rate at which budget authority becomes outlays in a fiscal year is called the spendout rate, or the *outlay rate*. The spendout rate varies among agencies' accounts depending on the timing of activity in each account.

Budget authority may be made available for obligation for a one-year, multi-year, or no-year period. One-year, or annual, budget authority is available for obligation only during a specific fiscal year, and any unobligated authority expires at the end of that fiscal year; multi-year budget authority is available for a period longer than one fiscal year; and no-year budget authority is available for an indefinite period.

Typically, new budget authority is provided in the form of permanent appropriations or annual appropriations. Permanent appropriations provide new budget authority each year without any annual legislative action. Usually, this type of new budget authority is provided in legislation authorizing the program, such as in the case of most entitlement programs (e.g., Social Security benefits). Annual appropriations, on the other hand, generally provide new budget authority for the particular fiscal year for which they were enacted. In some cases, new budget authority in annual appropriations acts is made available for more than one year, or for a future fiscal year. Annual appropriations are provided in the regular appropriations bills enacted by Congress and the President each year. Annual appropriations also may be provided in supplemental appropriations acts and continuing appropriations acts (often referred to as continuing resolutions).

New budget authority also may be made available to agencies in the form of borrowing authority, contract authority, and the authority to spend offsetting collections. Borrowing authority and contract authority allow agencies to borrow funds and enter into contracts prior to enactment of appropriations. Spending authority from offsetting collections, such as fees for certain market-oriented activities, may be provided to allow agencies to obligate and spend these funds. Offsetting collections are deducted from gross budget authority and outlays at the account or higher level.

REVENUES

Revenues, also known as *receipts*, are the funds collected from the public primarily as a result of the federal government's exercise of its sovereign powers. Most of the federal government's revenues consist of receipts from individual income taxes, social insurance (payroll) taxes, and corporate income taxes. Preferential provisions, such as tax exemptions, deductions, and credits, which reduce government receipts, are called *tax expenditures*. Excise taxes, duties, gifts, and miscellaneous receipts are other sources of federal revenues.

Offsetting collections are not classified as revenues, but instead are treated as negative spending (i.e., as noted above, deducted from gross budget authority and outlays).

BUDGET DEFICIT OR SURPLUS

The difference between government revenues and outlays in a fiscal year equals the *budget deficit* or *surplus*. A budget deficit results when outlays exceed revenues; a budget surplus results when revenues exceed outlays. What is counted as government revenues and outlays, however, depends on the presentation of the federal budget. The federal budget typically is presented in the form of the *unified budget*, reflecting a unified budget deficit or surplus. The unified budget, or *consolidated budget*, includes the revenues and outlays of all budget accounts, including federal funds and trust funds, regardless of whether they are designated in law as on-budget or off- budget. The unified budget represents a comprehensive picture of the federal government's financial activities.

The federal budget also is presented to distinguish between on-budget and off-budget accounts. That is, the federal budget also presents an *on-budget deficit or surplus* and an *off-budget deficit or surplus*. The on-budget deficit or surplus includes all accounts not designated in law as off- budget. The off-budget deficit or surplus includes those accounts designated in law as off-budget. Currently, there are three accounts designated in law as off-budget: the Federal Old-Age and Survivors Insurance Trust Fund (Social Security retirement), the Federal Disability Insurance Trust Fund (Social Security disability), and the Postal Service Fund.

Debt

The *gross federal debt*, almost all of which is subject to statutory limitation, consists of the *debt held by the public* plus the *debt held by government accounts*. The debt held by the public is the total net amount borrowed from the public by the federal government to cover its budget deficits over the years. Usually, analysts use the debt held by the public as the measure of the impact of the federal government's borrowing on the economy. It is this portion of federal debt that not only reflects the amount of the nation's wealth invested in federal government securities rather than in private investment, but also determines the level of real resources the government must acquire to make interest and principal payments. The debt held by government accounts is the total net amount of federal debt issued to specialized federal accounts, primarily trust funds. It represents internal transactions of the federal government.

In: United States Federal Budget Process
Editors: Gerard T. Brenner, et al.
ISBN: 978-1-61209-844-9

Chapter 7

FEDERAL BUDGET PROCESS REFORM IN THE 111TH CONGRESS: A BRIEF OVERVIEW

Megan Suzanne Lynch

SUMMARY

Procedural change is a recurrent feature of federal budgeting, although the scope and impact of changes may vary from year to year. In order to advance their budgetary, economic, or political objectives, both Congress and the President regularly propose and make changes to the federal budget process. This chapter briefly discusses the context in which federal budget process changes are made and identifies selected reform proposals by major category. The identification of reform proposals in this chapter is not intended to be comprehensive.

A variety of sources give rise to the interest in budget process reform, including Congress, the President, state and local government officials, and special commissions, among others. Congress initiated a thorough overhaul of its internal budget process and ameliorated ongoing conflicts with President Richard Nixon over the withholding of appropriated funds through enactment of the Congressional Budget and Impoundment Control Act of 1974. President Bill Clinton, like many Presidents before him, requested line-item veto authority, which Congress granted in 1996 in the Line Item Veto Act (but which was invalidated by court action in 1998). State and local government officials were instrumental in securing passage of the Unfunded Mandates

Reform Act of 1995. Finally, special commissions, such as the President's National Commission on Terrorist Attacks Upon the United States (the "9/11 Commission"), have recommended changes in budget structure and procedure that have been adopted.

The federal budget process is rooted in constitutional mandates, statutory requirements, House and Senate rules and practices, and administrative directives. Thus, there are several avenues through which budget process changes can occur. Either chamber may focus on changes in its rules, thereby minimizing the time needed to effect the change and the scale of potential conflict needed to be resolved, but at the same time possibly minimizing the impact of the changes. Broader and potentially more consequential changes, involving statutes or constitutional amendments, may entail a larger set of participants in the decision-making (i.e., the other chamber, the President, state legislatures), likely escalating the effort required to reach agreement and lengthening the time period before the changes take effect.

Legislative changes in the budget process may take the form of freestanding bills or joint resolutions (e.g., the Line Item Veto Act), or may be incorporated into other budgetary legislation, such as acts raising the debt limit (e.g., the Balanced Budget and Emergency Deficit Control Act of 1985, also referred to as the Gramm-Rudman-Hollings Act), implementing reconciliation instructions (e.g., the Budget Enforcement Act of 1990), or providing annual appropriations (e.g., revisions in the Senate's cap on discretionary appropriations). Budget process changes also may be included in the annual budget resolution (a concurrent resolution), or in simple House or Senate resolutions.

Procedural change is a recurrent feature of federal budgeting, although the scope and impact of changes may vary from year to year. To advance their budgetary, economic, or political objectives, both Congress and the President regularly propose and make changes to the federal budget process. This chapter briefly discusses the context in which federal budget process changes are made and identifies selected reform proposals by major category. The identification of reform proposals in this chapter is not intended to be comprehensive; other Congressional Research Service reports discuss different aspects of budget process reform in more detail.[1]

THE CONTEXT OF BUDGET PROCESS REFORM

Sources of Budget Process Reform Proposals

A variety of sources give rise to the interest in budget process reform, including Congress, the President, state and local government officials, and special commissions, among others. Congress initiated a thorough overhaul of its internal budget process and ameliorated ongoing conflicts with President Richard Nixon over the withholding of appropriated funds through enactment of the Congressional Budget and Impoundment Control Act of 1974. President Bill Clinton, like many Presidents before him, requested line-item veto authority, which Congress granted in 1996 in the Line Item Veto Act (but which was invalidated by court action in 1998). State and local government officials were instrumental in securing passage of the Unfunded Mandates Reform Act of 1995. Finally, special commissions, such as the President's National Commission on Terrorist Attacks Upon the United States (the "9/11 Commission"), have recommended changes in budget structure and procedure that have been adopted. (Citations to laws identified in this chapter are provided in the **Appendix**.)

Outside of Congress itself, the President probably has been the most important source of budget process reform proposals over the years. The President's annual budget submission to Congress typically includes at least several proposed changes in budget procedure.[2] In his final budget submission, for example, President George W. Bush advocated proposals involving such matters as enhanced controls over mandatory and discretionary spending, stricter standards for emergency spending designations, changes in how baseline calculations are made, earmark reform, line-item veto, biennial budgeting, a joint budget resolution, and an automatic continuing resolution.[3]

In late November 2008, President-elect Barack Obama signaled his interest in pursing budget process reform during the 111th Congress when he announced that he intended to nominate Peter Orszag to the position of director of the Office of Management and Budget (OMB) and Rob Nabors to the position of OMB deputy director. In making the announcement, President-elect Obama stated: "In these challenging times, when we are facing both rising deficits and a sinking economy, budget reform is not an option. It is an imperative."[4]

Perhaps more than any other factor over the years, concern about the size and persistence of the federal deficit has animated calls for budget process reform. The federal deficit, which amounted to $162 billion for FY2007 and $455 billion for FY2008, jumped to $1.414 trillion (9.9% of Gross Domestic Product) for FY2009 in the face of a significant economic downturn. In its January 2010 report presenting baseline budget projections, the Congressional Budget Office (CBO) estimated the baseline deficit at $1.3 trillion for FY2010 and $1.0 trillion for FY2011, and continuing at historically high levels through FY2020.[5]

The dramatic increase in the deficit, its likely persistence at high levels in the short term, and its unsustainable path in the long run, already has fueled strong interest in procedural reform. On January 14, 2009, several private organizations, including the Peter G. Peterson Foundation, the Pew Charitable Trusts, and the Committee for a Responsible Federal Budget, announced a joint enterprise (the Peterson-Pew Commission on Budget Reform) to foster changes in the budget process.[6]

The next day, President-elect Obama stated in an interview with the *Washington Post* that he would convene a "fiscal responsibility summit" prior to submitting the FY2010 budget to Congress, focusing on control of long-term obligations for entitlement programs.[7] The summit was held on February 23, 2009, and included a session on budget process reform in which, among other issues, the notion of different types of commissions to formulate long-term budget solutions was addressed.[8] (The following year, President Obama created the National Commission on Fiscal Responsibility and Reform by executive order, as discussed later in this chapter.)

In his budget submission for FY2010, President Obama pledged to cut the deficit in half by the end of his first term and asked Congress to act on various changes in the budget process that would, in part, contribute to this goal. The proposed changes included, among other things, restoration of the statutory "pay-as-you-go" requirement (with significant modifications), expedited legislative procedures for the consideration of certain presidential rescission proposals, and a limit on advance appropriations; similar proposals were included in his FY2011 budget.[9]

Avenues of Reform

The federal budget process is rooted in constitutional mandates, statutory requirements, House and Senate rules and practices, and administrative directives.[10] Thus, there are several avenues through which budget process changes can occur. Either chamber may focus on changes in its rules, thereby minimizing the time needed to effect the change and the scale of potential conflict needed to be resolved, but at the same time possibly minimizing the impact of the changes. Broader and potentially more consequential changes, involving statutes or constitutional amendments, may entail a larger set of participants in the decision-making (i.e., the other chamber, the President, state legislatures), likely escalating the effort required to reach agreement and lengthening the time period before the changes take effect.

Legislative changes in the budget process may take the form of freestanding bills or joint resolutions (e.g., the Line Item Veto Act), or may be incorporated into other budgetary legislation, such as acts raising the debt limit (e.g., the Balanced Budget and Emergency Deficit Control Act of 1985, also referred to as the Gramm-Rudman-Hollings Act), implementing reconciliation instructions (e.g., the Budget Enforcement Act of 1990), or providing annual appropriations (e.g., revisions in the Senate's cap on discretionary appropriations).[11] Budget process changes also may be included in the annual budget resolution (a concurrent resolution), or in simple House or Senate resolutions.

In some years, changes made in the budget process were comprehensive. The Budget and Accounting Act of 1921 established the executive budget process, the Congressional Budget Act of 1974 created the congressional budget process, and the Balanced Budget and Emergency Deficit Control Act of 1985 and the Budget Enforcement Act of 1990 imposed additional budget controls on a temporary basis. In other years, such as 1987, 1993, and 1997, existing budget process statutes were modified in a less comprehensive fashion and extended for limited periods. At other times, Congress and the President enacted statutes changing only selected aspects of the budget process; the Line Item Veto Act (of 1996) is one example. Finally, in every Congress, the House and Senate have modified existing rules and practices affecting the budget process and sometimes instituted new ones.

Like other types of legislation, statutes making changes in the budget process are subject to review by the judiciary. In several major instances, the Supreme Court has declared procedures established by Congress and the President to be invalid on constitutional grounds. The one-House legislative veto (found in many acts, including the Impoundment Control Act of 1974), for example, was invalidated by *I.N.S. v. Chadha* in 1983, 103 S.Ct. 715 (1983); the triggering of a sequester by the Comptroller General under the Gramm-Rudman-Hollings Act was invalidated by *Bowsher v. Synar* in 1986, 478 U.S. 714 (1986); and the Line Item Veto Act was invalidated by *Clinton v. City of New York* in 1998, 118 S.Ct. 2091 (1998). In the wake of court decisions, Congress and the President may successfully modify legislation (e.g., 1987 legislation modifying the Gramm-Rudman-Hollings Act, vesting the authority to trigger a sequester in the OMB director), but sometimes persistent efforts to enact corrective legislation do not succeed (e.g., line-item veto proposals).

Given that nearly every committee of the House and Senate has jurisdiction over legislation with a budgetary impact, interest in the budget process and proposals to change it radiate throughout both chambers. Although jurisdiction over executive and congressional budget procedures generally resides with the Budget, Oversight and Government Reform, and Rules Committees in the House, and with the Budget, Homeland Security and Governmental Affairs, and Rules and Administration Committees in the Senate, other House and Senate committees, particularly the appropriations and tax committees, may exert influence over budget process changes affecting their legislative interests.

Initial Budget Process Changes in the 111th Congress

The first opportunity in a new Congress to change budget procedures usually occurs on the first or second day of session. The House, which unlike the Senate is not a continuous body, must adopt its rules anew at the beginning of each Congress. Traditionally, the House adopts its rules from the previous Congress, with modifications (that may include changes in the budget process), in the form of a simple resolution.

On January 6, 2009, the House adopted the opening-day rules package for the 111th Congress, H.Res. 5, by a vote of 242-181. The measure included several changes in the budget process, including modifications to the "pay-as-you-go" rule and earmarking rules that had been adopted at the beginning of the 110th Congress.[12] Some of the specific changes made by H.Res. 5 are discussed below under the applicable areas of reform.

A second opportunity for budget process changes typically comes in March and April, when the two chambers consider the annual budget resolution for the fiscal year beginning on October 1. Under authority referred to as the "elastic clause" (in Section 301 of the 1974 Congressional Budget Act), either chamber may include procedural provisions in the annual budget resolution that are consistent with the purposes of the 1974 act.

Various procedural provisions were incorporated into the FY20 10 budget resolution (S.Con.Res. 13), on which the House and Senate reached final agreement on April 29, 2009, principally in a separate title (Title IV—Budget Process). These provisions included House and Senate restrictions on the use of advance appropriations and emergency designations, procedures to adjust budget levels to accommodate program integrity initiatives, and a Senate point of order pertaining to short-term deficits.[13]

Congress also may express its interest in the budget process in venues that do not involve legislative activity. In the past, consideration in the Senate of nominations to the position of OMB director and deputy director often has afforded the opportunity to discuss budget process reforms.[14] Nominations to the position of OMB director and deputy director are considered, pursuant to S.Res. 445 (108th Congress), by both the Senate Budget Committee and the Senate Homeland Security and Governmental Affairs Committee.

The Senate Budget Committee and the Senate Homeland Security and Governmental Affairs Committee held hearings on January 13 and January 14, 2009, respectively, regarding President- elect Obama's choices for director (Peter Orszag) and deputy director (Rob Nabors) of OMB. The prospective nominees discussed the need to review a variety of budget process reform proposals, addressing such concerns as the growth of entitlement spending over the long run and the need to better integrate budgeting and performance evaluation activities in OMB.[15]

Both President Obama and Congress continued to address budget process reform in 2010, during the second session of the 111th Congress. As previously mentioned (and discussed below), President Obama created the National Commission on Fiscal Responsibility and Reform by executive order, and the President and Congress enacted a major procedural reform into law, the Statutory Pay-As-You-Go Act of 2010 (also discussed below). The consideration of other budget process reforms is pending.

SELECTED BUDGET PROCESS REFORM PROPOSALS

Among the various budget process reform proposals that have been or may be considered during the 111th Congress, many pertain to categories such as internal "pay-as-you-go" (PAYGO) rules in the House and Senate; restoration of the statutory discretionary spending limits and PAYGO process; earmarking; and modifications to budget resolution, reconciliation, and appropriations processes. To illustrate the diversity of proposals, these and other categories of reform are discussed briefly below.

PAYGO Rules and Discretionary Spending Limits

Statutory Enforcement Procedures

From 1991 through 2002, federal budget legislation was constrained by statutory limits on discretionary spending and a PAYGO requirement for direct spending (sometimes referred to as mandatory spending) and revenue legislation.[16] Both of these budget constraints were established by the Budget Enforcement Act of 1990, which amended the Balanced Budget and Emergency Deficit Control Act of 1985. The discretionary spending limits and the PAYGO requirement were enforced by sequestration, a process by which violations were remedied by automatic, across-the- board spending cuts. These statutory budget constraints were extended in 1993 and 1997 (and further modified by other legislation), but the discretionary spending limits expired at the end of FY2002 and the PAYGO requirement effectively was terminated in December 2002.

In recent years, there has been considerable interest in restoring, and possibly making significant modifications to, the statutory enforcement procedures. Some observers have argued that the budget enforcement mechanisms associated with the Budget Enforcement Act promoted fiscal discipline throughout the 1990s, and contributed to the federal government achieving a total budget surplus in FY1998—the first in almost 30 years—and the following three fiscal years.

With the return of sizeable deficits in the short term due to economic decline and in the long term due principally to the growth of Medicare, Medicaid, and Social Security, some have argued for restoring such statutory mechanisms to strengthen fiscal discipline. A principal point of contention with regard to the PAYGO requirement has been whether it should apply to revenue legislation. While some maintain that revenue reductions should not face the hurdle of a statutory PAYGO requirement because they are needed to fuel growing revenues, others assert that accommodating further revenue reductions in a PAYGO requirement (i.e., by applying it only to direct spending) likely would undermine efforts to achieve significant deficit reduction, in part by encouraging some spending initiatives to be reformulated as revenue-losing provisions.

The FY2008 and FY2009 budget resolutions included sense-of-the-Congress statements that a statutory PAYGO requirement should be reinstated to help control the deficit (Section 508 of S.Con.Res. 21 and Section 515 of S.Con.Res. 70, respectively), but the 110th Congress did not take any action in this regard.

On June 9, 2009, President Obama announced that he would submit a PAYGO proposal to Congress, the Statutory Pay-As-You-Go Act of 2009, that would restore a process applying to both direct spending and revenue legislation.[17] The House responded to the President's proposal first, passing a bill (H.R. 2920) the following month and incorporating it into several other measures toward the end of the session. In January 2010, the Senate added a statutory PAYGO proposal to a measure increasing the debt limit (H.J.Res. 45); the House concluded action on the measure in early February, and President Obama signed it into law on February 12, 2010, as P.L. 111-139, the Statutory Pay-As-You-Go Act of 2010 (Statutory PAYGO Act).[18]

The Statutory PAYGO Act establishes a process intended, as Section 2 of the act states, "to enforce a rule of budget neutrality on new revenue and direct spending legislation." The budgetary effects of revenue and direct spending provisions enacted into law, including both costs and savings, are recorded by the OMB director on two PAYGO scorecards covering rolling 5-year and 10-year periods (i.e., in each new session, the periods covered by the scorecards roll forward one fiscal year).[19] The budgetary effects of PAYGO measures are determined by statements inserted into the *Congressional Record* by the chairmen of the House and Senate Budget Committees and referenced in the measures. As a general matter, the statements are expected to reflect cost estimates prepared by CBO. If this procedure is not followed for a PAYGO measure, then the budgetary effects of the measure are determined by OMB.

Shortly after a congressional session ends, OMB finalizes the two PAYGO scorecards and determines whether a violation of the PAYGO requirement has occurred (i.e., if a debit has been recorded for the budget year on either scorecard). If so, the President issues a sequestration order that implements largely across-the-board cuts in nonexempt direct spending programs sufficient to remedy the violation by eliminating the debit. Many direct spending programs and activities are exempt from sequestration. If no PAYGO violation is found, no further action occurs and the process is repeated during the next session.

In the case of the statutory limits on discretionary spending, one issue has been the period of time for which they should be established. Advocates of two- or three-year limits argue that the five- year framework employed earlier leads to limits that are too unrealistic in the later years (due to changing circumstances). Limits that are unrealistically high fail to impose discipline, while limits that are unrealistically low encourage evasions through gimmickry and other means. Shorter-term limits, they argue, are more apt to be realistic and effective constraints on spending.

During the 111th Congress, the Senate has considered, but rejected, several amendments (offered by Senators Jeff Sessions and Claire McCaskill) that would have established discretionary spending limits as part of the Congressional Budget Act of 1974.

House and Senate PAYGO Rules

As a supplement to the statutory PAYGO requirement, the Senate established its own PAYGO rule in 1993 as a provision in the FY1994 budget resolution.[20] The rule, which operates differently than the statutory requirement, has been modified several times.

Over the years, several unsuccessful efforts were made to establish a PAYGO rule in the House. A PAYGO rule was contained in the House's rules package for the 110th Congress, in Section 405 of H.Res. 6. Title IV was considered separately and adopted by the House on January 5, 2007, by a vote of 280-152 (all five titles of H.Res. 6 were adopted by the House and took effect on that day). The House's PAYGO rule imposes a bar against revenue and direct spending legislation that increases a deficit (or reduces a surplus) over different time periods (i.e., the 6-year and 11-year periods beginning with the current fiscal year).

In May 2007, the Senate revised its PAYGO rule as part of the FY2008 budget resolution (Section 201 of S.Con.Res. 21). The revised Senate rule conforms closely to the House rule, applying to the same two time periods and eliminating any exception for revenue or direct spending proposals assumed in the budget resolution; it expires on September 30, 2017. In addition, the revised Senate PAYGO rule is buttressed by other Senate rules designed to discourage legislation that increases the deficit in both the short and long terms; these rules can be waived only by the affirmative vote of three-fifths of the membership (60 Senators, if no seats are vacant).

The implementation of the House and Senate PAYGO rules in the 110th Congress was associated with considerable controversy regarding issues of compliance and the need to effectively waive the rules for the consideration of some major legislation, especially bills dealing with the housing crisis and economic downturn in a manner that substantially increases the deficit in the short term. In response to some of these concerns, modifications to the House PAYGO rule were included in Section 2(j) of H.Res. 5, which was adopted on January 6, 2009. The changes include (1) an alignment with the Senate PAYGO rule so that both Houses use the same CBO baseline for enforcement; (2) a procedure to allow one House-passed measure to pay for spending in a separate House-passed measure, if the two are linked at the engrossment stage;

and (3) a procedure for designating in legislation emergency exceptions to the rule.[21]

Earmarking

Reform of congressional earmarking practices in appropriations, direct spending, and tax legislation (and accompanying reports) was addressed by the House and Senate with the adoption of new rules in 2007, during the 110th Congress. Some changes in earmark rules and practices occurred at the beginning of the 111th Congress, as discussed below, and additional reforms in this area continue to be examined.

Although definitions of earmarking vary, an earmark generally is considered to be an allocation of resources to specifically targeted beneficiaries, either through earmarks of discretionary or direct spending, limited tax benefits, or limited tariff benefits. Earmarks may be proposed by the President or may be originated by Congress. Concern about recent earmarking practices arose because some of them were inserted into legislation or accompanying reports without any identification of the sponsor, and the belief that many earmarks were not subject to proper scrutiny and diverted resources to lesser-priority items or items without sufficient justification, thereby contributing to wasteful spending or revenue loss.

The essential feature of earmark reform proposals is a bar against the consideration of legislation that does not identify individual earmarks and the Members who sponsored them, the distribution of such information in a way that makes it readily available before the legislation is considered, and certification by earmark sponsors that neither they nor their spouses have a financial interest in the earmark.

Earmark reform provisions, requiring the identification of earmarks and their sponsors before legislation may be considered and imposing other restrictions on the use of earmarks, were contained in Title IV (Section 404) of the House's rules package for the 110th Congress, H.Res. 6, adopted on January 5, 2007. The earmark reform provisions were added to the rules of the House as Clause 9 of Rule XXI and Clauses 16 and 17 of Rule XXIII. The earmark identification requirement applies to all legislation; if no earmarks are included, then a statement to that effect must be supplied.

Later in the session, on June 18, 2007, the House adopted H.Res. 491, a measure dealing (for the remainder of the 110th Congress) with the consideration of conference reports on regular appropriations acts containing earmarks that were not submitted to the conference by either chamber. The measure established a point of order intended to curtail the practice of "air-dropping" earmark provisions, not first passed by either chamber, into appropriations acts at the conference stage. The point of order is disposed of by the question of consideration.

On January 18, 2007, the Senate adopted S. 1, ethics reform legislation. Title I of the act, referred to separately as the Legislative Transparency and Accountability Act of 2007, included earmark reform provisions requiring the prior identification of earmarks, and their sponsors, in all spending and revenue legislation, and various other constraints on earmarking practices. Senator Robert C. Byrd, the chairman of the Senate Appropriations Committee, announced on April 17 that the committee would follow a policy of requiring earmark disclosure for the FY2008 appropriations cycle, similar to the requirements set forth in S. 1, pending further action on the measure.

On July 31, 2007, the House passed S. 1 with an amendment under the suspension of the rules procedure, by a vote of 411-8. The Senate agreed to the House amendment, by a vote of 83-14, on August 2, thus clearing the measure. President George W. Bush signed the bill into law on September 14, 2007, as P.L. 110-8 1 (121 Stat. 735-776), the Honest Leadership and Open Government Act of 2007. In its final form, P.L. 110-81 included earmark reform provisions in Section 521 (Congressionally Directed Spending), which were added to the Standing Rules of the Senate as a new Rule XLIV.

At the beginning of the 111th Congress, on January 6, 2009, the chairmen of the House and Senate Appropriations Committees, Representative David Obey and Senator Daniel Inouye, jointly announced further changes in earmark practices. The changes, which took effect for FY20 10 appropriations acts, included (1) a requirement that Members post information on their earmark requests at the time they are made; (2) the dissemination of earmark disclosure tables at the time of subcommittee action; and (3) a reduction of earmarks to 50% of the FY2006 level for nonproject-based accounts and a cap at 1% of discretionary spending in subsequent years.[22]

In addition, on January 6, 2009, the House also adopted changes in its earmark rules as part of its action on H.Res. 5. Section 2(i) of the resolution incorporated the prohibitions of H.Res. 491 of the prior Congress (restricting the use of "air-dropped" earmarks) into Clause 9 of House Rule XXI.

In March 2010, Chairman Obey and Chairman Inouye announced that the earmark policies applicable to the FY20 10 appropriations acts would be continued into the FY20 11 appropriations cycle.[23] The House Appropriations Committee also imposed a ban on earmarks for for-profit companies. Further,

House Minority Leader John Boehner announced, on March 11, 2010, that the Republican Conference had agreed that day to a unilateral moratorium on all earmarks for FY2011, including tax- and tariff-related earmarks.[24] (House Republicans had rejected a short- term earmark moratorium in late 2008, but created a special 10-member panel to examine further earmark reforms in 2009.)[25]

Congressional Budget Resolution and Reconciliation

The Congressional Budget Act of 1974 requires the House and Senate to adopt a budget resolution each year, setting forth aggregate spending and revenue levels, and spending levels by major functional categories, for at least five fiscal years. The budget resolution, which is a concurrent resolution and therefore does not become law, provides an overall budget plan that guides congressional action on individual spending, revenue, and debt-limit measures. The 1974 act includes an optional reconciliation procedure that provides for the development and consideration of revenue, spending, and debt-limit legislation to carry out budget resolution policies; enforcement of budget resolution policies also occurs by means of various points of order that may be raised on the floor. Budget resolutions and reconciliation measures are considered under expedited procedures in both chambers.

Some Members of Congress, as well as the President, have argued that the budget resolution would be more effective in enforcing budget policy by making it a joint resolution requiring the President's approval. A joint budget resolution would directly involve the President in congressional actions on the budget early in the process. If the President and Congress reach an impasse on a joint budget resolution, however, some are concerned that action on spending and revenue bills might be significantly delayed.

In the Senate, a 50-hour limit on the consideration of a budget resolution applies under the expedited procedures. When the time limit expires, many amendments may still be pending; they are brought up for disposition by vote but without any time left to debate them, a situation referred to as "vote-arama." The Senate typically ameliorates the consequences of a "vote-arama" by allowing a minimal amount of debate time (e.g., two minutes per side) for each amendment under unanimous consent, but proposals have been offered in past Congresses in an effort to eliminate "vote-aramas" altogether. The Senate Budget Committee examined the phenomenon of "vote-arama" and other issues relating to the consideration of budget resolutions in a hearing on February 12, 2009.[26]

During the 1 980s and much of the 1 990s, reconciliation was used principally as a means of reducing the deficit. While some reconciliation measures included spending increases or revenue reductions, the net impact of the legislation was to reduce the deficit. In recent years, the reconciliation process has been used mainly to expedite the passage of legislation that increases the deficit, primarily through revenue reduction.

Some Members in the House and Senate have argued that the reconciliation process should be altered so that it may be used only to reduce the deficit. As part of the changes in the budget process included in the rules package for the 110th Congress, H.Res. 6, the House included a ban (in Section 402) against the consideration of a budget resolution containing reconciliation directives that would increase the deficit or reduce the surplus over the six-year or 11-year periods beginning with the current fiscal year. The Senate included a similar ban for the same two time periods in the FY2008 budget resolution (Section 202 of S.Con.Res. 21).

Because reconciliation legislation is considered in the Senate under expedited procedures, with a 20-hour time limit for debate, the issue of "vote-arama" applies as well. The proposals offered in the past to deal with this situation with respect to the consideration of budget resolutions also have applied to the consideration of reconciliation bills.

Annual Appropriations Process

Discretionary spending, which amounts to more than one-third of federal spending, is provided each year in regular, supplemental, and continuing appropriations acts. Discretionary spending funds most of the routine operations of federal agencies.

Considerable attention was focused during the past two Congresses on Appropriations Committee structure. At the beginning of the 109th Congress, the House and Senate Appropriations Committees consolidated and realigned their subcommittees in order to streamline the appropriations process, facilitate the timely enactment of appropriations bills, and minimize the likelihood of using consolidated appropriations acts. Both committees disbanded their VA-HUD Subcommittee, and the House Appropriations Committee disbanded two others (District of Columbia and Legislative Branch), leaving 12 Senate and 10 House appropriations subcommittees.

At the start of the 110th Congress, further adjustments in subcommittee alignments of the House and Senate Appropriations Committees were made, leaving each committee with 12 subcommittees. Among the changes made, each committee established a Financial Services and General Government Subcommittee and the House Appropriations Committee reestablished a Legislative Branch Subcommittee.

Later during the 110th Congress, the House adopted H.Res. 35, a measure establishing a Select Intelligence Oversight Panel of the House Appropriations Committee. The panel is charged with studying and reviewing intelligence activities and the intelligence budget and making recommendations in this area; it does not exercise jurisdiction over appropriations legislation for these purposes. The panel includes members of the House Appropriations Committee and the House Permanent Select Committee on Intelligence. This action represented the House's response to one of the recommendations of the 9/11 Commission. Although the Senate may address the commission's recommendation with respect to intelligence activities in the 111th Congress, no further major realignments in subcommittee structure of either committee are expected at this time.

When a regular appropriations act or a continuing resolution is not in place after the start of the fiscal year on October 1, an agency does not have the legal authority to incur obligations in order to function and must shut down, resulting in the furlough of federal employees and disruptions in service. To prevent a government shutdown (or the threat of one) due to the expiration of funding, some Members have proposed establishing an automatic continuing resolution. An automatic continuing resolution would provide an uninterrupted source of funding for discretionary activities in the event one or more regular appropriations acts are not enacted by the start of a new fiscal year. Although such a device could eliminate or reduce employee furloughs and service disruptions, some view an automatic continuing resolution as substituting a formulaic response for deliberate and informed decision making.

Item Veto/Expanded Rescission Authority

When a spending or revenue act is sent to the President for his consideration, he must approve or veto the measure in its entirety. After a spending measure has become law, the President may impound funds through rescission, which cancels the funding, or deferral, which delays the expenditure of funds. Congress exercises its responsibilities in this area through procedures established under the Congressional Budget and Impoundment Control Act of 1974 and the regular legislative process.

Advocates of greater budget discipline proposed the Line Item Veto Act, which became law in 1996 (P.L. 104-130) but was struck down by the Supreme Court on June 25, 1998, in *Clinton v. City of New York*, 118 S.Ct. 2091 (1998). Under this act, the President was authorized to strike individual items of discretionary spending, direct spending, and certain limited tax benefits in any law.

In the years following the Supreme Court decision, various proposals have been made in Congress to grant item veto authority to the President in a manner that passes constitutional muster or to otherwise expand his rescission powers. President George W. Bush, in 2006, proposed a "legislative line-item veto," under which Congress would have to consider proposed rescissions in an expedited manner. The House passed H.R. 4890, the Legislative Line Item Veto Act of 2006, on June 22, 2006, by a vote of 247-172; the Senate did not act on the measure. The Senate considered a legislative line-item veto proposal in the 110th Congress, in the form of an amendment offered by Senator Judd Gregg, first to S. 1 and then to minimum wage legislation, H.R. 2; in both instances, the Gregg amendment ultimately was withdrawn.

As part of the budget process proposals included in his FY20 10 and FY20 11 budget submissions, President Obama asked Congress to establish expedited legislative procedures for the consideration of certain rescission proposals offered by the President. On May 28, 2010, Representative John Spratt introduced the President's proposal as H.R. 5454, the Reduce Unnece-ssary Spending Act of 2010.

Although advocates of the item veto or expanded rescission powers for the President contend that such tools will enhance budgetary discipline, critics suggest that their usefulness for budgetary discipline is overstated and that they may adversely affect the balance of power between Congress and the President over budget decisions.

Commission/Task Force on Long-Term Budgetary Issues

Considerable attention has been focused recently on the large imbalances projected in the federal budget over the long term, particularly with respect to the Social Security, Medicare, and Medicaid programs. One device advocated by some as a means of compelling action on longterm budgetary issues is a bipartisan commission or task force empowered to recommend legislative changes that would correct or mitigate the imbalances.[27]

Advocates of the commission or task force approach argue that it would be an effective means of surmounting political opposition and achieving an end result because of the bipartisan nature of the group, the avoidance of preconditions with respect to policy options (i.e., all options would be "on the table"), and the action-forcing nature of expedited legislative procedures. Adherents to the use of regular legislative procedures to deal with these issues maintain that while they may entail a more time-consuming and difficult route, they afford more openness and participation in the decision-making process and are more likely to lead to widespread acceptance of the results.

During the 110th Congress, a leading example of such a proposal was the Bipartisan Task Force for Responsible Fiscal Action Act of 2007 (S. 2063, introduced by Senators Kent Conrad and Judd Gregg, and H.R. 3655, introduced by Representatives Jim Cooper and Frank Wolf). The bill would have established a bipartisan, 16-member task force (including the Treasury Secretary and another member from the executive branch, and seven members each from the House and Senate). The task force would have been charged with developing legislative recommendations (by December 9, 2008) to significantly improve the long-term balances in the federal budget, including the balances in Social Security and Medicare; the recommendations would have needed to be approved by at least 12 of the task force members. Under the proposal, the recommendations would have been considered by the House and Senate during the 2009 congressional session (during the first year of the new presidential administration), under expedited legislative procedures that would limit consideration to 100 hours in each chamber and bar amendments.[28]

In the 111th Congress, Representatives Cooper and Wolf introduced a measure recommending a similar approach—H.R. 1557, the Securing America's Future Economy Commission Act, also referred to as the SAFE Commission Act; the bill was introduced in the Senate by Senator George Voinovich as S. 1056. Senators Conrad and Gregg did not immediately introduce their Bipartisan Task Force bill, but advocated its approach in the media.[29]

On November 10, 2009, the Senate Budget Committee held a hearing on the matter, "Bipartisan Process Proposals for Long-Term Fiscal Stability."[30] Senators Conrad and Gregg introduced S. 2853, the Bipartisan Task Force for Responsible Fiscal Action Act of 2009, on December 9, 2009.

On January 26, 2010, during consideration of the debt-limit measure (H.J.Res. 45) that became the vehicle for the Statutory PAYGO Act of 2010, competing amendments to establish a Bipartisan Task Force for Responsible Fiscal Act, offered by Senator Kent Conrad and Judd Gregg (S.Amdt. 3302) and Senator Max Baucus (S.Amdt. 3306), were considered. The vote on the Conrad-Gregg amendment was 53-46, and having failed to secure the minimum 60 votes required by a unanimous consent agreement, it was withdrawn; the second amendment, offered by Senator Baucus, was withdrawn by unanimous consent without a vote.

Following the Senate's rejection of the Conrad and Baucus amendments, President Obama elected to create a commission by executive order. On February 18, 2010, the President signed Executive Order 13531, creating the National Commission on Fiscal Responsibility and Reform.[31] Under the executive order, the commission "is charged with identifying policies to improve the fiscal situation in the medium term and to achieve fiscal sustainability over the long run." The commission must vote no later than December 1, 2010, on a final report regarding recommendations to achieve its mission, and at least 14 affirmative votes are required for the final report to be issued. With a membership composed of 18 members—10 Democrats and 8 Republicans—the 14-vote threshold ensures that any recommendations issued by the commission would be supported by at least half the members from each party.

Capital Budgeting

Unlike many states, the federal government does not employ separate capital and operating budgets; instead, all revenue and spending is merged together into a "unified" budget. Information on capital budgeting, however, has been provided for many years as a separate chapter in one of the volumes of the President's budget. Interest in adopting a capital budget for the federal government has been examined from time to time. In 1999, a commission established by President Bill Clinton pursuant to Executive Order 13037 (March 3, 1997), the President's Commission to Study Capital Budgeting, recommended several changes in budgetary practice but did not recommend the adoption of a formal capital budget.

Advocates of capital budgeting generally regard it as a means of boosting resources for infrastructure needs (e.g., surface transportation and aviation systems struggling to meet capacity and deteriorating water infrastructure), overcoming an alleged bias against capital spending in the current budget process, and rationalizing decision-making in this area. Critics of capital budgeting assert that shifting a significant portion of the budget to an accrual basis (in which costs are apportioned over the lifetime of an asset rather than accounted for up front) would unduly complicate the budget process and undermine the task of setting priorities over the full range of governmental activities.

As a first step toward improved budgeting for infrastructure needs, some have advocated more information gathering and analysis in this area. One proposal introduced in the 110th Congress, for example, would have created a bipartisan National Commission on the Infrastructure of the United States charged with studying, among other things, "the methods used to finance the construction, acquisition, rehabilitation, and maintenance of public works improvements (including general obligation bonds, tax-credit bonds, revenue bonds, user fees, excise taxes, direct governmental assistance, and private investment)."

Biennial Budgeting

While many authorizations are enacted on a multiyear cycle, Congress acts on budget resolutions and appropriations acts annually. Biennial budgeting proposals would change the cycle under which Congress acts on budget resolutions and appropriations acts (and annual authorization acts) to two years.

Biennial budgeting proposals are intended to reduce the amount of time Congress spends on budgetary legislation, to allow more time for congressional oversight of federal agencies and programs, and generally to provide for more efficient budget decision-making. In the view of some, however, a biennial approach could impair Congress's ability to respond quickly to changing economic and budgetary circumstances.

APPENDIX. CITATIONS TO SELECTED BUDGET PROCESS LAWS

Budget and Accounting Act of 1921

P.L. 67-13; June 10, 1921; 42 Stat. 20-27.

Budget and Accounting Procedures Act of 1950

P.L. 81-784; September 12, 1950; 64 Stat. 832-845.

Congressional Budget and Impoundment Control Act of 1974

P.L. 93-344; July 12, 1974; 88 Stat. 297-339.

Balanced Budget and Emergency Deficit Control Act of 1985

Title II of P.L. 99-177 (Increasing the Statutory Limit on the Public Debt); December 12, 1985; 99 Stat. 1038-1101.

Balanced Budget and Emergency Deficit Control Reaffirmation Act of 1987

Title I of P.L. 100-119 (Increasing the Statutory Limit on the Public Debt); September 29, 1987; 101 Stat. 754-784.

Budget Enforcement Act of 1990

Title XIII of P.L. 101-508 (Omnibus Budget Reconciliation Act of 1990); November 5, 1990; 104 Stat. 1388-573 through 630.

Omnibus Budget Reconciliation Act of 1993

P.L. 103-66; August 10, 1993; 107 Stat. 683-685 (Title XIV).

Unfunded Mandates Reform Act of 1995

P.L. 104-4; March 22, 1995; 109 Stat. 48-71.

Line Item Veto Act

P.L. 104-130; April 9, 1996; 110 Stat. 1200-1212.

Budget Enforcement Act of 1997

Title X of P.L. 105-33 (Balanced Budget Act of 1997); August 5, 1997; 111 Stat. 677-7 12.

Statutory Pay-As-You-Go Act of 2010

Title I of P.L. 111-139; February 12, 2010; 124 Stat. 8-30.

Notes: Major portions of selected budget process laws are codified as follows:

- 2 U.S.C. 621, et seq. (Congressional Budget and Impoundment Control Act of 1974, as amended);
- 2 U.S.C. 900, et seq. (Balanced Budget and Emergency Deficit Control Act of 1985, as amended); and
- 31 U.S.C. 1101, et seq. (Budget and Accounting Act of 1921, as amended).

For additional information on these and other budget process laws, see CRS Report RL30795, *General Management Laws: A Compendium*, by Clinton T. Brass et al..

End Notes

[1] CRS reports on different budget process reforms are listed under the appropriate terms under "Current Legislative Issues" on the CRS homepage; other pertinent CRS reports may be accessed in several ways, including by subject term and author searches on the CRS homepage. Also, see CRS Report RL3 1478, *Federal Budget Process Reform: Analysis of Five Reform Issues*, by James V. Saturno, for a discussion of selected reforms proposed in past years.

[2] In recent years, the President's budget process reform proposals have been included in a separate chapter of the *Analytical Perspectives* volume.

[3] See the Office of Management and Budget, *Budget of the United States Government, Fiscal Year 2009, Analytical Perspectives*, February 4, 2008, Chapter 15 (Budget Reform Proposals), pp. 2 15-225.

[4] The Office of the President-Elect, "President-elect Barack Obama announces Office of Management and Budget Director and Deputy Director," press release, November 25, 2008, available on the Obama transition website at http://change.gov/newsroom.

[5] Congressional Budget Office, *The Budget and Economic Outlook: Fiscal Years 2010 Through 2020*, January 2010, Summary Table 1 (CBO's Baseline Budget Outlook), p. xii.

[6] Information regarding the commission may be found on the websites of the organizations, at http://www.pgpf.org, http://www.pewtrusts.org, and *http://www.newamerica.net/programs /fiscal_policy*

[7] Michael D. Shear, "Obama Pledges Entitlement Reform," *Washington Post*, January 16, 2009, p. A-1.

[8] Activities during the summit are summarized in The White House, *Fiscal Responsibility Summit*, March 20, 2009; see the discussion of budget process reform on pp. 28-33. The report is available on the White House website at http://www.whitehouse.gov/assets

[9] See the Office of Management and Budget, *Budget of the United States Government*: (1) *Fiscal Year 2010, Analytical Perspectives*, May 7, 2009, Chapter 15 (Budget Reform Proposals), pp. 2 15-220; and (2) *Fiscal Year 2011, Analytical Perspectives*, February 1, 2010, Chapter 13 (Budget Process), pp. 143-155.

[10] For an overview of the federal budget process, see CRS Report 98-721, *Introduction to the Federal Budget Process*, by Robert Keith.

[11] A comprehensive listing and description of major budget process laws enacted over the past century (and full legal citations to them) is provided in CRS Report RL3 0795, *General Management Laws: A Compendium*, by Clinton T. Brass et al.

[12] For a detailed discussion of these changes in the budget process, see CRS Report RL34 149, *House Rules Changes Affecting the Congressional Budget Process Made at the Beginning of the 110th Congress*, by Bill Heniff Jr.

[13] The House and Senate reached final agreement on the FY20 10 budget resolution by agreeing to the conference report on S.Con.Res. 13 (H.Rept. 111-89; April 27, 2009), by a vote of 233-193 in the House and 53-43 in the Senate.

[14] During the 1 10th Congress, for example, the Senate considered the nomination of Jim Nussle to be OMB director, confirming his appointment on September 4, 2007 (by a vote of 69-24). Although budget process changes were not a prominent part of the debate in committee and on the floor, a PAYGO requirement and other procedural matters were discussed briefly.

[15] Kerry Young, "Orszag to Suggest Program Cuts in February Budget Outline," *CQ Today*, January 14, 2009; and Jonathan Nicholson, "OMB Chief-Designate Orszag Plans February Budget Outline Submission," Bureau of National Affairs, *Daily Report for Executives*, January 14, 2009.

[16] The statutory PAYGO process in effect during that period is explained in CRS Report R41005, *The Statutory PAYGO Process for Budget Enforcement: 1991-2002*, by Robert Keith.

[17] The legislative text of the proposal, along with a section-by-section summary and related documentation, is provided on the OMB website at *http://www.whitehouse.go v/omb/news_060909_paygo/*.

[18] For a summary and legislative history of the act, see CRS Report R41157, *The Statutory Pay-As-You-Go Act of 2010: Summary and Legislative History*, by Robert Keith.

[19] The PAYGO scorecards are available on the OMB website at *http://ww w.whitehouse.gov/omb/paygo_default/*. Through the end of May 2009, the 5-year scorecard showed a credit in excess of $4 billion and the 10-year scorecard showed a credit in excess of $16 billion.

[20] An overview of statutory and rules-based PAYGO procedures is provided in CRS Report RL34300, *Pay-As-You-Go Procedures for Budget Enforcement*, by Robert Keith.

[21] The changes are explained in "Section-by-Section of Rule Changes – 111th Congress," undated, available on the Democratic website of the House Rules Committee at http://www.rules11 1_hres_ruleschnge_smmry.pdf.

[22] House Appropriations Committee, "House and Senate Appropriations Committees Announce Additional Reforms in Committee Earmark Policy," press release, January 6, 2009, available on the committee's website at http://appropriations

[23] See (1) House Appropriations Committee, "Recent History of Earmark Reform," fact sheet, March 2010; and (2) Senate Appropriations Committee, "Senate Appropriations Committee Policy on Earmarks," press release, March 11, 2010.

[24] See (1) Jackie Kucinich, "GOP Adopts Sweeping Earmark Ban," *Roll Call*, March 11, 2010, and (2) Edward Epstein and David Clarke, "House Republicans Embrace One-Year Moratorium on Earmarks," *CQ Today*, March 11, 2010.

[25] See (1) David Clarke and Alan K. Ota, "House GOP Backs Away from Earmark Moratorium," *CQ Today*, November 20, 2008; and (2) Catharine Richert, "House Republicans Create Anti-Earmark Panel," *CQ Today*, December 19, 2008.

[26] Access to a video of the hearing and the prepared statements of witnesses is available on the Senate Budget Committee (Majority) website at *http://budget.senate.gov/democratic /hearingstate.html*.

[27] For background on this issue, see CRS Report R40986, *Proposals for a Commission to Address the Federal Government's Long-Term Fiscal Situation*, coordinated by Clinton T. Brass, Matthew Eric Glassman, and Jacob R. Straus.

[28] The proposal was explained by Senators Conrad and Gregg in the *Congressional Record* (daily ed.), September 18, 2007, pp. S11662-S11665.

[29] See Kent Conrad and Judd Gregg, "A Fiscal Battle on Two Fronts," *Washington Post*, January 5, 2009, available on the Senate Budget Committee website at *http://budget.senate .gov/democratic/documents/2009/* Wash%20Post_A%20Fiscal%20Battle.pdf.

[30] A video presentation of the hearing is available on the website of the Senate Budget Committee at http://www.senate.gov/fplayers/CommPlayer/commFlashPlayer.cfm?fn=budget111009&st=870.

[31] *Federal Register*, vol. 75, no. 35, Tuesday, February 23, 2010, "National Commission on Fiscal Responsibility and Reform," pp. 7927-7928. The commission's website is*http://w ww.fiscalcommission.gov/*.

In: United States Federal Budget Process ISBN: 978-1-61209-844-9
Editors: Gerard T. Brenner, et al.

Chapter 8

THE FY2011 FEDERAL BUDGET

Mindy R. Levit

SUMMARY

While considering the FY2011 budget, Congress faces very large budget deficits, rising costs of entitlement programs, and significant spending on overseas military operations. In FY2008 and FY2009, the enactment of financial intervention and fiscal stimulus legislation helped to bolster the economy, though it increased the deficit. While GDP growth has returned in recent quarters, unemployment remains elevated and government spending on "automatic stabilizer" programs, such as unemployment insurance and income support, remains higher than historical averages.

Between FY2000 and FY2009, federal spending accounted for approximately 20% of the economy (GDP) and federal revenues averaged 18% of GDP. In FY2009, the U.S. government spent almost $3.5 trillion (25% of GDP) and collected $2.1 trillion in revenue (15% of GDP). Between FY2008 and FY2009, outlays increased by $535 billion, while revenues fell by $419 billion. The deficit in FY2009 was $1,413 billion, or 9.9% of GDP, sharply higher than deficits in recent years.

The current economic climate poses a challenge to policymakers shaping the federal budget. Numerous actions taken by the federal government in FY2008 and FY2009 have had major effects on the budget, including two major economic stimulus measures and a variety of programs within the

Federal Reserve, Treasury, and Federal Deposit Insurance Corporation (FDIC). The impact of this legislation, along with any additional legislation enacted, will influence deficit levels in FY20 10 and beyond. The final costs of federal responses to this turmoil will depend on the pace of economic recovery, how well firms with federal credit guarantees weather future financial shocks, and government losses or gains on its asset purchases.

While many economists concur on the need for short-term fiscal stimulus despite adverse impact on the deficit, concerns remain about the federal government's long-term fiscal situation. Rising costs of federal health care programs and baby boomer retirements present further challenges to fiscal stability. Operating these programs in their current form may pass substantial economic burdens to future generations.

The Obama Administration released its FY2011 budget on February 1, 2010. The main policy initiatives emphasized in the President's Budget include the creation of a fiscal commission tasked with improving the fiscal stability over the long term, other deficit-reduction proposals, ongoing economic recovery, and a continuation of health care reform, clean energy, and education initiatives.

On April 22, 2010, the Senate Budget Committee reported the FY2011 budget resolution (S.Con.Res. 60) by a vote of 12-10. The resolution provided for revenue levels of $1,838 billion and outlays of $3,191 billion in FY2011 for a deficit of $1,260 billion, or approximately 8.4% of GDP. On July 1, 2010, the House adopted a budget enforcement resolution (H.Res. 1493), which established top line discretionary spending levels for FY20 11 for House appropriators.

This chapter provides an historical overview of the budget trends through the most recently completed fiscal year (2009). It discusses major budgetary challenges over the past several fiscal years given the current economic conditions and provides an in-depth discussion of the FY2011 budget process. Finally, it provides context for the issues facing the country's federal budget over the long term.

The federal budget is central to Congress's ability to exercise its "power of the purse." Federal budget decisions express Congress's priorities and reinforce Congress's influence on federal policies. Making budgetary decisions for the federal government is an enormously complex process and requires balancing competing goals.[1] Recent economic turmoil has strained the federal budget as a result of declining revenues and increasing spending levels. As recovery continues, the budget process will allow the President and

Congress to negotiate and refine spending plans for the nation's fiscal priorities over the longer term.

The federal government faces very large budget deficits, rising costs of entitlement programs, and significant spending on overseas military operations. The enactment of financial intervention and fiscal stimulus legislation in FY2008 and FY2009 helped to bolster the economy, though it increased the budget deficit. These federal interventions and policy responses, unprecedented in recent decades, helped stimulate economic activity and reduced dislocation in financial markets, but also exposed the federal government to credit risks.

While GDP growth has returned in recent quarters, unemployment remains elevated and government spending on "automatic stabilizer" programs, such as unemployment insurance and income support, remains higher than historical averages.[2] This suggests that the recession's effects on the budget will likely linger for several more fiscal years.

In addition to the current challenges, concerns remain about the federal government's long-term fiscal situation. The rising costs of federal health care programs and the effects of the baby boom generation's retirement present serious challenges to future fiscal stability. Operating these programs in their current form may pass on substantial economic burdens to future generations, which may require significant government action and public sacrifice at levels greater than those needed to counteract the recent economic downturn.

OVERVIEW

Budget Cycle

A single year's budget cycle takes roughly three calendar years from initial formation by the Office of Management and Budget (OMB) until final audit.[3] The executive agencies begin the budget process by compiling detailed budget requests in the calendar year before the President's budget submission. Many agencies start working on their budgets during the spring and summer—about a year and a half before the fiscal year begins. OMB oversees the development of these agency requests. The President, by law, must submit a budget, which is based on OMB's work, by the first Monday in February.[4]

Congress typically begins formal consideration of the budget resolution once the President submits his budget request. The budget resolution sets out a plan, agreed to by the House and Senate, that establishes the framework for subsequent budget legislation. Because the budget resolution is a concurrent resolution, it is not sent to the President for approval.

House and Senate Appropriations Committees and their subcommittees typically begin reporting discretionary spending bills after the budget resolution is agreed upon. Appropriations Committees review agency funding requests and propose levels of budget authority (BA). Appropriations acts passed by Congress set the amount of BA available for specific programs and activities. Authorizing committees, which control mandatory spending, and committees with jurisdiction over revenues also play important roles in budget decision making.

During the fiscal year, which begins on October 1, Congress and OMB oversee the execution of the budget. Once the fiscal year ends on the following September 30, the Treasury Department and the Government Accountability Office (GAO) begin year-end audits.

Revenues, Outlays, and Deficits for FY2009

Between FY2000 and FY2009, federal spending has accounted for approximately 20% of the economy (as measured by gross domestic product—GDP) and federal revenues averaged 18% of GDP. In FY2009, the U.S. government spent almost $3.5 trillion and collected $2.1 trillion in revenue.[5] Between FY2008 and FY2009, outlays increased by $535 billion while revenues fell by $419 billion (in nominal terms), leading to the upward and downward spikes in outlays and revenues, respectively, shown in **Figure 1**.

The annual differences between revenue (i.e., taxes and fees) that the government collects and outlays (i.e., spending) result in the budget deficit (or surplus).[6] The total deficit in FY2009 was $1,413 billion, or 9.9% of gross domestic product (GDP), sharply higher than deficits in recent years. While large by historical standards, the FY2009 deficit was somewhat smaller than many analysts had originally forecasted at the start of FY2009 because several of the economic recovery programs, which, cost less than anticipated.[7]

The total deficit, according to some budget experts, gives an incomplete view of the government's fiscal condition because it includes Social Security surpluses (which are held in Treasury trust funds until used to pay future benefits).[8] Excluding off-budget items (Social Security benefits paid net of Social Security payroll taxes collected and the U.S. Postal Service's net balance) the on-budget FY2009 federal deficit was $1,551 billion.

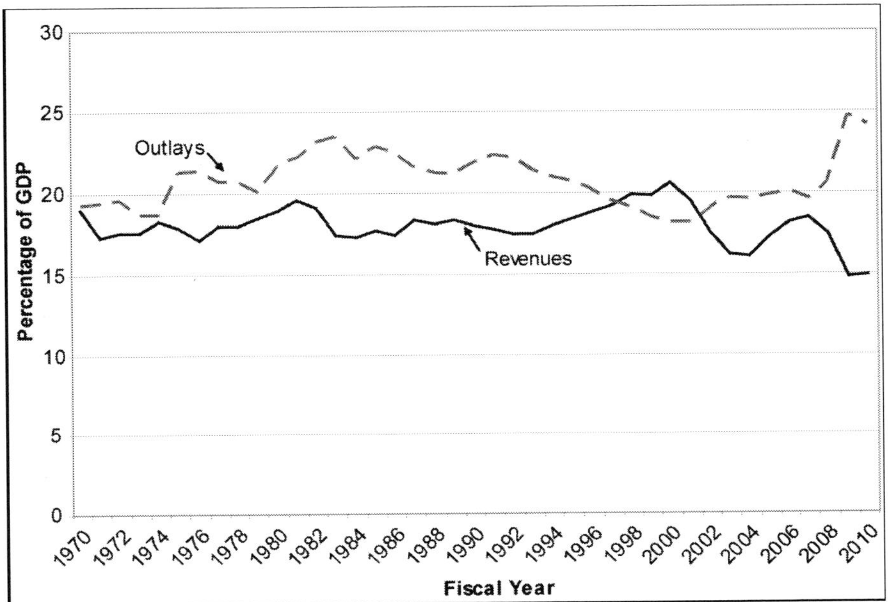

Source: CBO, Historical Tables, available at *http://www.cbo.gov/budget/historical.shtml;* Budget Projections, available at *http://www.cbo.gov/budget/budproj.shtml*. Figures for FY20 10 are estimated.

Figure 1. Total Outlays and Revenues as a Percentage of GDP, FY1 970-FY20 1 0.

Trends

Federal Spending

Budget enforcement legislation divides federal outlays into discretionary and mandatory spending, as well as net interest.[9] Discretionary spending is controlled by annual congressional appropriations acts. Mandatory spending encompasses spending on entitlement programs and spending controlled by laws other than annual appropriation acts. Net interest comprises the government's interest payments on debt held by the public, offset by small amounts of interest income the government receives from certain loans and investments. Total outlays rose from 20.7% of GDP in FY2008 to 24.7% of GDP in FY2009.

Entitlement programs such as Social Security, Medicare, and Medicaid make up the bulk of mandatory spending.[10] Other mandatory spending programs include Temporary Assistance to Needy Families (TANF),

Supplemental Security Income (SSI), unemployment insurance, veterans' benefits, federal employee retirement and disability, SNAP (formerly Food Stamps), and refundable tax credits, such as the Earned Income Tax Credit (EITC). Congress sets eligibility requirements and benefits for entitlement programs, rather than appropriating a fixed sum each year. Therefore, if the eligibility requirements are met for a specific mandatory program, outlays are made automatically.[11]

Over the past 40 years, mandatory spending has taken up a larger and larger share of the federal budget. In 1962, before the creation of Medicare and Medicaid, less than 30% of all federal spending was mandatory. By FY2009, mandatory spending had grown to 60% of total outlays, with Social Security, Medicare, and the federal share of Medicaid alone comprising almost 41% of all federal spending.

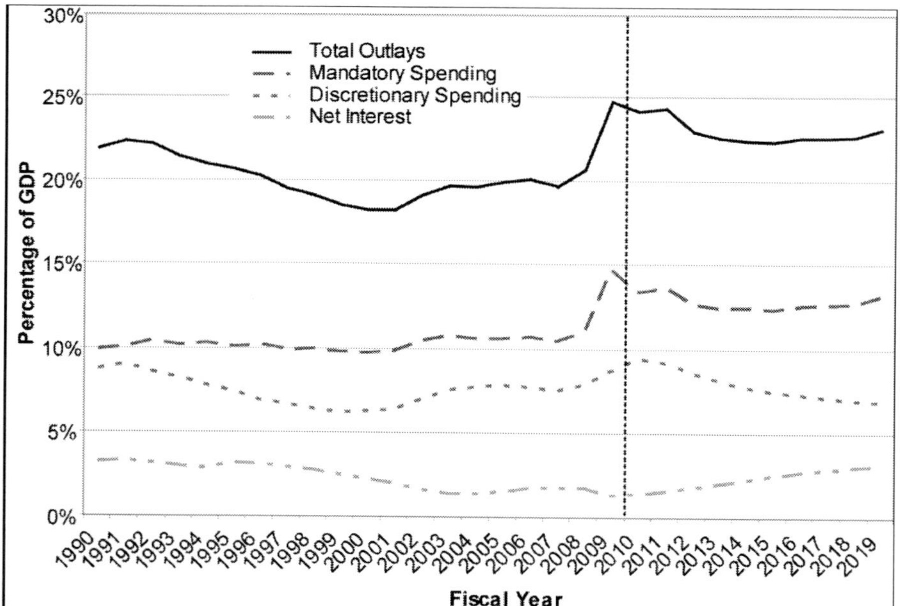

Source: CBO, Historical Tables, available at http://www.cbo.gov/budget/historical.shtml and Budget Projections, January 2010, available at http://www.cbo.gov/budget/budproj.shtml. Data for FY20 10 are estimates and data for FY20 11 -FY2020 are projections.

Figure 2. Outlays by Type as a Percentage of GDP, FY1 990-FY2020.

As **Figure 2** shows, mandatory spending, which equaled 11.0% of GDP in FY2008, totaled 14.7% of GDP in FY2009. TARP spending, costs linked to the federal conservatorship of Fannie Mae and Freddie Mac, and certain provisions of the American Recovery and Reinvestment Act of 2009 (ARRA), accounted for much of this increase in mandatory spending. Under current law, CBO projects that FY2020 mandatory spending will total 13.3% of GDP, incorporating a return to economic stability but the beginning of long-term growth in entitlement spending.

Discretionary spending as a share of GDP rose from 6.3% of GDP in FY2000 to 8.7% of GDP in FY2009 (see **Figure 2**), increasing 4.5% a year on average in real terms. The share of discretionary spending as a proportion of total federal outlays rose from 34.4% in FY2000 to 35.2% in FY2009. On average, from FY2000 to FY2009, defense discretionary outlays grew 5.3% per year in real terms, largely due to operations in Iraq and Afghanistan, while real nondefense discretionary outlays grew 3.6% per year.

By FY2020, according to CBO's baseline projections (which assume that discretionary spending remains constant in real terms), discretionary spending will fall to 6.7% of GDP, close to its levels in the late 1990s.[12] Net interest payments accounted for 1.3% of GDP in FY2009 and are estimated to rise to 3.2% of GDP in FY2020.[13]

Because discretionary spending represents slightly more than one-third of total federal outlays, some budget experts contend that any significant reductions in federal spending must include mandatory spending cuts. Other budget and social policy experts contend that cuts in mandatory spending would cause substantial disruption to many households because mandatory spending funds important parts of the social safety net. Nevertheless, there is widespread agreement that action is needed to bring down anticipated high debt and deficit levels to restore long-term fiscal health.[14]

Federal Revenue

Individual income taxes have long been the largest source of federal revenues, followed by social insurance (payroll) taxes. Federal individual and corporate income tax revenues typically track broader trends in the economy. In FY2008, individual income tax revenues totaled $1,146 billion (7.9% of GDP), comprising about 45% of total federal revenues. In FY2009, difficult economic conditions and the tax relief provisions of ARRA led individual income tax revenue to fall to $915 billion (6.4% of GDP). Corporate income tax revenues fell from $304 billion in FY2008 to $138 billion in FY2009. Federal revenues from other sources fell as well, although much less dramatically.[15] It is likely that revenues will remain depressed in FY20 10. The longer-term revenue outlook depends on the speed of economic recovery and the legislative actions of Congress on certain expiring tax provisions and potential tax reform.[16]

Deficits, Debt, and Interest

The federal government's fiscal stance is often gauged by the annual budget deficit. The budget deficit, however, may give a partial and potentially misleading picture of the government's longterm fiscal condition. [17] Annual budget deficits or surpluses determine, over time, the level of federal debt and affect the growth of interest payments to finance the debt.

Federal Deficits

Differences between revenues and outlays determine whether or not the budget is in surplus or deficit. Occasional deficits, in and of themselves, are not necessarily problematic. Deficit spending can allow governments to smooth outlays and taxes to shield taxpayers and program beneficiaries from abrupt economic shocks in the short term. Persistent deficits, however, lead to growing levels of federal debt that may lead to higher interest payments, tax increases, or spending cuts, and may also have adverse macroeconomic consequences in the long term.[18]

Deficit projections for the next several fiscal years are high relative to historic standards. The deficit reached its peak in FY1943 at 30.3% of GDP. After WWII, deficits remained relatively low until the mid-1980s. In FY1985, the deficit reached 6.0% of GDP. The FY2009 total deficit was $1,413 billion (9.9% of GDP), the largest in proportion to GDP since FY1945.[19]

Federal Debt and Debt Limit

Gross federal debt is composed of debt held by the public and intragovernmental debt.[20] Intragovernmental debt is the amount owed by the federal government to other federal agencies, to be paid by the Department of the Treasury. This amount largely consists of money contained in trust funds, such as Social Security, that has been invested in federal securities as required by law.[21] Debt held by the public is the total amount the federal government has borrowed from the public and remains outstanding. This measure is generally considered to be the most relevant in macroeconomic terms because it is the debt sold in credit markets.

Changes in debt held by the public generally track the movements of the annual on-budget deficits and surpluses. Whether or not the movements of gross federal debt will follow those of debt held by the public depends on how intragovernmental debt changes.[22] Higher debt levels could slow investment and lower economic growth.[23]

Congress sets a ceiling on federal debt through a legislatively established limit that helps Congress assert its constitutional prerogative to control spending. The debt limit also imposes a form of fiscal accountability that compels Congress and the President to take visible action, in the form of a vote authorizing a debt limit increase, to allow further federal borrowing when nearing the statutory limit. The debt limit, however, can hinder the Treasury's ability to manage the federal government's finances when the amount of federal debt approaches this ceiling. In those instances, the Treasury has had to take unusual and extraordinary measures to meet federal obligations.[24] While the debt limit has never caused the federal government to default on its obligations, it has caused inconvenience and uncertainty in Treasury operations at times.

At the end of FY2009, federal debt subject to limit was approximately $11,853 billion, of which $7,544 billion was held by the public. CBO estimates that debt held by the public will reach $8,797 billion at the end of FY2010, with debt subject to limit totaling $13,260 billion.[25] The debt limit was most recently raised on February 12, 2010 (P.L. 111-139), and currently stands at $14,294 billion.[26]

Net Interest

In FY2009, the United States spent $187 billion, or 1.3% of GDP, on net interest payments on the debt.[27] Since FY1970, the U.S. spent an average of 2.2% of GDP on interest payments. What the government pays in interest depends on market interest rates as well as on the size and composition of the federal debt. Currently, low interest rates have held net interest payments as a percentage of GDP below the historical average despite increases in borrowing to finance the deficit. Some economists, however, have expressed concern that federal interest costs could rise sharply once the economy recovers, resulting in future strain on the budget.[28]

Budgeting in Tough Economic Times

The current economic climate poses another major challenge to policymakers shaping the federal budget. Numerous actions taken by the federal government in FY2008 and FY2009 have had major effects on the budget. Federal spending tied to means-tested social programs has also been increasing due to rising unemployment, while federal revenues have fallen as individuals' incomes drop and corporate profits sink. Additional legislative action and the pace of economic recovery could continue to impact deficit levels.

Federal Response to Economic and Financial Market Turmoil

The federal government has responded to financial turmoil with an extraordinary set of measures, including two major economic stimulus measures and a variety of programs within the Federal Reserve, Treasury, and Federal Deposit Insurance Corporation (FDIC). In February 2008, Congress enacted a $152 billion package (P.L. 110-185, Economic Stimulus Act of 2008) to stimulate consumption by sending refunds to taxpayers and letting firms depreciate their capital more quickly.

Another effort to jump-start economic growth came in the form of a second stimulus package signed into law by President Obama on February 17, 2009. The American Recovery and Reinvestment Act of 2009 (ARRA; P.L. 111-5) included provisions that are now estimated to total $862 billion in increased discretionary and mandatory spending and reduced tax revenue over the FY2009-FY2019 period.[29] ARRA contains support for state and local governments in the form of increased transportation project, Medicaid, and school funding, funding for health care information technology, extended unemployment benefits, as well as tax cuts and rebates among other provisions.[30]

In addition to these stimulus efforts, various governmental bodies, through legislative and existing authority, engaged in numerous financial stability programs. The federal government placed government-sponsored enterprises Fannie Mae and Freddie Mac into conservatorship in September 2008, thereby gaining temporary authority to provide unlimited funds if necessary to help them remain solvent. In October 2008, Congress passed the Emergency Economic Stabilization Act of 2008 (EESA; P.L. 110-343), which authorized the Treasury Secretary to use $700 billion (subject to certain congressional restrictions and notifications) to purchase troubled assets through the Troubled Assets Relief Program (TARP). As part of this program, Treasury purchased preferred shares from banks, assisted AIG and the domestic automakers, and provided other assistance to financial institutions. The Federal Reserve created a panoply of lending facilities, to provide financial institutions with loans in exchange for various types of collateral. The FDIC has used its standing authority to resolve failed banks and administer the federal guarantees on individual deposits, in addition to carrying out a broad guarantee program on debt issued by banks and supporting joint interventions in large banks.[31]

In response to this financial instability, Congress enacted the Dodd-Frank Wall Street Reform and Consumer Protection Act (P.L. 111-203) on July 21, 2010.[32] This legislation, which contains various provisions under a new regulatory umbrella, has minimal budgetary impact and is therefore beyond the scope of this chapter.[33]

Changing Budgetary Impact of Major Financial Interventions and Economic Recovery Programs

The size, variety, and complexity of federal responses to financial and economic turmoil present many challenges to budget analysis. The ultimate costs of these responses will depend on how the economy performs, how well firms with federal credit guarantees weather future financial shocks, and whether or not government funds are ultimately repaid. Estimating how much these responses will cost the federal government is difficult, both for conceptual and operational reasons. As a result, estimates of the costs of some of these programs have already changed significantly.

The distinction between outlays and budget authority is important to understanding the budgetary consequences of federal responses to economic and financial turmoil. Outlays are disbursed federal funds. Budget authority, as determined by what Congress appropriates, is what federal agencies can legally spend. Budget authority has been compared to funds deposited into a checking account, which then can be used for federal spending. Until the federal government disburses funds to make purchases, however, no outlays occur.

This distinction is especially important in understanding the impact of ARRA on the budget deficit over the next several fiscal years. The programmatic costs of ARRA consisted of roughly one-quarter revenue reduction measures and three-quarters increased outlays. Outlay measures can affect the budget deficit more slowly than revenue or transfer measures due to the time it takes between obligation of funds and actual spending (or outlays) on specific projects or programs. For example, if an individual receives extended unemployment benefits under the provisions of ARRA, the budgetary cost to the government would be incurred almost immediately upon the benefit being issued to the individual. However, if a state receives a grant to fund a transportation project, which may take five years to complete, the entire grant amount will be obligated immediately while the budgetary impact will be felt in each of the five years as outlays are made until the project is completed.[34]

Estimating the precise budgetary impact of programs like TARP and the government's conservatorship of Fannie Mae and Freddie Mac (also known as government sponsored enterprises or GSEs) is difficult for different reasons. Early amounts of TARP funds were used to purchase preferred equity stakes in major banks. EESA requires those equity purchases to be recorded in the budget in the year acquired on a net present value basis with an adjustment for market risk, so that the future sale of those equity stakes would offset much of the cost of acquiring them.[35] Over time, improved market conditions, lower estimates of the amount of TARP authority needed, and bank repurchases of stock sold to the government have decreased the impact of the program on the budget deficit. Other assets that have been acquired through TARP are treated similarly.

Differences also exist in the cost estimates of OMB and CBO due to the use of alternative assumptions and interpretations of budget concepts. OMB estimates TARP outlays on a net present value basis over the FY2009-FY20 19 period at $127 billion (excluding administrative costs and interest effects). CBO estimates the value of these net present value outlays at $109 billion (excluding administrative expenses) over the FY2009-FY2019 period.[36] The deficit impact of this program only tells part of the story. TARP purchases have had a different impact on the level of federal debt than they have had on the deficit. Though the impact of TARP on the deficit for the FY2009-FY20 19 period is now estimated by CBO to be $109 billion in net costs over the period, as discussed above, outlays by Treasury have been significantly greater than that. As of the end of FY2009, Treasury had disbursed $365.1 billion.[37] In order to finance these outlays, the Treasury had to sell debt to the public. Taking this and other adjustments into account, the increase in federal debt held by the public exceeded the deficit in FY2009. However in FY2010, CBO estimates that the increase in the federal debt held by the public will be lower than the deficit.[38]

Estimating the cost of the aid given to the GSEs, in budgetary terms, is also complex. Unlike TARP, no legislation stipulated the precise methodology with which to use when accounting for the budgetary impact of these interventions. Prior to conservatorship, federally chartered Fannie Mae and Freddie Mac were considered non-governmental entities, which essentially meant that their balance sheets were not included in budget totals. Subsequent to the Treasury Secretary taking control of these entities through conserve-atorship, CBO determined that they were now part of the government and should be reflected in the federal budget. At that point, CBO began recording these costs on a net cash flow basis, similar to what is used to calculate TARP's budgetary impact. OMB, however, takes a different approach and records cash outlays to the GSEs in the budget but does not include any additional amount to account for market risk. These differences led to big discrepancies in budgetary impact since OMB only records liabilities as they occur, while CBO accounts for future shortfalls on these financial commitments now.

The differences between the accounting methodologies used by OMB and CBO lead to divergent effects on the budget. CBO recorded a subsidy cost of $291 billion in FY2009. OMB placed the budgetary cost for the GSE intervention in FY2009 at $95.6 billion in cash outlays. Over the FY2010-FY2019 period, OMB projects that cash outlays to the GSEs will total an additional $65 billion. Over the same period, CBO projects a subsidy cost of $99 billion.[39] OMB has faced criticism for its methodology as some argue that they do not account for the full budgetary cost of the program. Once the fiscal year ends, CBO uses the figures recorded by OMB.

Budget Deficit Estimates for FY2010

The CBO baseline estimates the FY2010 budget deficit at $1,368 billion or 9.4% of GDP, slightly lower than the FY2009 deficit of $1,413 billion (9.9% of GDP).[40] The deficit is projected to be slightly lower than that of FY2009 due to an anticipated decline in federal aid to the financial sector, offset by increases in outlays from ARRA, income support programs, and net interest. Though revenues are expected to increase slightly, the slow pace of economic recovery will continue to hold receipts well below their historical average.

Under the President's Budget, deficit estimates for FY2010 amount to $1,556 billion or 10.6% of GDP. This is larger than CBO's baseline deficit estimate due to differences in assumptions used as well as the inclusion of the impact of certain legislation not yet enacted. Some of these proposals include indexing the alternative minimum tax to inflation, the inclusion of a jobs initiatives and other temporary recovery measures, preventing a reduction in Medicare physician payments, tax cuts for families and businesses, and additional spending on overseas contingency operations.[41]

On July 23, 2010, OMB released its Mid-Session Review, which provided updated estimates of the FY2010 spending, revenue, and deficit levels. The Administration now estimates that the FY2010 deficit will total $1,471 billion or 10% of GDP, about $84 billion less than what was estimated in February. The change in the deficit estimate is due to lower than anticipated federal outlays of about $118 billion, primarily for unemployment compensation, deposit insurance, and non-defense discretionary spending. Revenue collections in FY2010 are also estimated to be about $33 billion less than estimated in February.[42] The changes in the budget deficit estimate primarily result from revisions in economic factors, rather than changes in policy.

Healthcare Legislation

Congress acted on one of the Obama Administration's major budgetary initiatives by enacting the Patient Protection and Affordable Care Act (PPACA; P.L. 111-148) and the Health Care and Education Reconciliation Act of 2010 (HCERA; P.L. 111-152), which were signed into law on March 23 and March 30, 2010, respectively. Among other provisions, this legislation established a mandate for most U.S. residents to obtain health insurance, set up insurance exchanges, expanded Medicaid, and imposed various tax code changes.[43] Together, the spending and revenue measures contained in the PPACA and HCERA are estimated to increase the deficit by $6 billion in FY2010, but are projected to reduce the deficit by $143 billion over the FY20 1 0-FY20 19 period.[44] The Administration believes that health care reform is critical to economic recovery and stabilizing the federal government's long-run fiscal condition.[45] Additional legislative action affecting health care programs may be necessary over the long term.

FY2010 Supplemental Legislation

Supplemental appropriations complicate the budget process, specifically when it comes to comparing baseline budget forecasts due to the terms of budget enforcement conventions. CBO's baseline presumes that discretionary spending levels will continue as enacted for the following fiscal years in real (i.e., inflation adjusted) terms. If baseline projections are made before Congress enacts supplemental legislation, the baseline is likely to understate the likely cost of discretionary spending in future years. If the baseline projections are made after enactment of supplemental legislation and supplemental funding is lower in future years, then they could overstate the deficit estimates in future years. A measure to extend temporarily the period of eligibility for certain direct assistance benefits has already been enacted. Notable measures on war funding, job creation, and longer-term benefit extensions are now being considered by Congress.

War Funding[46]

Thus far, Congress has provided a total of $135.6 billion in FY2010 funding for overseas contingency operations, including $128.8 billion for the Defense Department, $4.8 billion for the State Department and USAID, and $2.0 billion for the VA. FY2009 funding levels for overseas contingency operations totaled $155.1 billion. With his budget, President Obama included a request for an additional $35.1 billion in FY20 10 supplemental funding for these operations. On July 29, 2010, the President signed the Supplemental Appropriations Act, 2010 (P.L. 111-212), which included the funding that he requested for overseas contingency operations, as well as funding for FEMA disaster relief, activities related to the Deepwater Horizon Oil spill, and other measures.[47]

Hiring Incentives to Restore Employment Act and Other Measures

On December 16, 2009, the House passed the Jobs for Main Street Act (H.R. 2847), which provided approximately $154 billion in funding for infrastructure investment, public service jobs, and emergency relief for families.[48] The Senate passed a scaled-down version of this legislation, titled Hiring Incentives to Restore Employment Act, on February 24, 2010, that would provide tax credits for hiring and retaining unemployed workers, extend a tax provision in ARRA related to expensing for small businesses, and reauthorize certain transportation authorities. A modified version of the Senate bill was agreed to and was signed by the President on March 18, 2010 (P.L. 111-147). Together, the spending and revenue measures in the modified bill would increase the deficit by $4.5 billion in FY2010, but are projected to reduce the deficit by $0.7 billion over the FY20 1 0-FY2020 period.[49]

In subsequent legislation, the President signed the Temporary Extension Act of 2010 on March 2, 2010 (H.R. 4691, P.L. 111-144), which provided an extension of some direct assistance provisions including unemployment benefits and COBRA subsidies, along with an increase in Medicare payments to physicians and certain revenue raisers. Subsequent legislation extended the eligibility period for unemployment compensation and Medicare physician payment increases through November 30, 2010 (P.L. 111-157 and P.L. 111-205; P.L. 111-192).[50]

Budget Baseline Projections

Given the increasing calls for attention on the country's fiscal health and in light of the current economic conditions and long term outlook, future projections of budget deficit levels are garnering even greater attention. Due to the nature of projections, slight changes in assumptions can lead to large effects in outyear totals. Therefore, it is important to understand what projections include and assume.

CBO computes baseline projections using assumptions set out in budget enforcement legislation.[51] Forecasts based on these assumptions typically yield higher revenue estimates and slower growth of discretionary spending relative to scenarios independent forecasters consider likely. More specifically, CBO baseline projections incorporate three legislatively mandated assumptions: that discretionary spending remains constant in inflation-adjusted terms, that the 2001 and 2003 tax cuts fully expire after 2010 (as current law specifies), and that one-year "patches" to the alternative minimum tax (AMT) will lapse even though past Congresses have extended AMT patches year after year. However, CBO does provide projections of these costs separately from its baseline. In addition to these legislative assumptions, macroeconomic assumptions, namely the point at which CBO expects the recession to end and the speed of the recovery, will also affect the baseline estimates and projections, especially given the current economic climate.

Baseline projections showed substantial growth in receipts after 2010, when most of the tax cuts from 2001 and 2003 expire. Federal deficits are expected to grow rapidly beyond the 10-year forecast window unless major policy changes are made, however, largely because of increased outlays due to rapidly growing health care costs and baby boomer retirements.

Budget Fiscal Year 2011

The Obama Administration released its FY20 11 budget on February 1, 2010. Congress began its consideration of the FY20 11 budget after receiving the President's budget request.

Obama Administration FY2011 Budget

The Administration's FY20 11 budget contains six volumes: (1) *The Budget*; (2) *Historical Tables*; (3) *Analytical Perspectives*; (4) *Appendix*; (5) *Terminations, Reductions, and Savings*; and (6) *Supplemental Materials*.[52] These documents lay out the Administration's projections of the fiscal outlook for the country, along with spending levels proposed for each of the federal government's departments and programs. The *Historical Tables* volume also provides significant amounts of budget data, much of which extends back to 1962 or earlier.

Consistent with the presentation of the FY20 10 budget, the Obama Administration provided three separate deficit projections.[53] First, OMB projected a Budget Enforcement Act (BEA) baseline, using methods that mirror those CBO uses to project its current-law baseline. The BEA baseline assumes that discretionary spending remains constant in real (i.e., inflation-adjusted) terms, the 2001 and 2003 Bush Administration tax cuts expire at the end of 2010, and that the alternative minimum tax (AMT) will not be "patched."[54] Many budget analysts believe such projections offer an overly rosy scenario of the long-term budget picture. Under this scenario, the FY20 11 deficit is projected to total $912 billion.

The Obama Administration also projected a Current Policy Baseline, which in its view, provides a more transparent and realistic reflection of the federal government's current fiscal situation. They use this methodology as a base for understanding how new policy choices affect the fiscal outlook, essentially replacing the current BEA baseline. The Administration's Current Policy Baseline assumes that the 2001 and 2003 tax cuts will be extended, that the alternative minimum tax (AMT) will be "patched" to reflect the 2009 parameter, and that certain Medicare physician payments will not be cut. This baseline also includes an adjustment for the conversion of Pell Grants from discretionary to mandatory spending. The deficit under this scenario is projected to reach $1,145 billion in FY2011.

The final deficit projection, the Proposed Budget, illustrates the impact on the budget outlook if all of the policies of the Obama Administration are implemented. In FY20 11, the Administration projects that the deficit would reach $1,267 billion. Both the Current Policy Baseline and the Proposed Budget project deficits throughout the 10-year budget window, with deficits peaking in FY2010. Under the Proposed Budget, the deficit would fall from 8.3% of GDP in FY2011 to 3.6% of GDP by FY20 18, before rising to 4.2% of GDP in FY2020.[55]

In his budget for FY20 11, President Obama also presented a wide-ranging policy agenda. The main policy initiatives he emphasized include the creation of a fiscal commission tasked with improving the fiscal stability over the long term; other deficit reduction proposals; ongoing economic recovery; and clean energy and education initiatives.

Fiscal Commission

President Obama's priorities included the creation of a fiscal commission tasked with balancing the budget excluding net interest payments by FY20 15. (This is also referred to as a primary deficit of zero.) The commission's recommendations would lead to annual budget deficits of roughly 3% of GDP, the projected amount of interest payments in FY20 15. Obama's proposed budget, which does not take into account any potential recommendations of the fiscal commission, recommends deficit levels averaging 4.5% of GDP over the FY20 1 1-FY2020 period. This means that, on average, the commission would need to recommend spending decreases, tax increases, or some combination of each, totaling 1.5% of GDP. After FY2020, the policy changes needed to balance the budget, excluding net interest, will likely be higher as health care costs continue to rise.

By executive order, President Obama created the 18-member commission on February 18, 2010. The commission comprises 12 sitting members of Congress, appointed by Senate and House leaders, and 6 additional members appointed by the President. The recommendations of the commission must be submitted to Congress by December 1, 2010, with 14 out of 18 votes needed to report recommendations.[56]

Other Deficit Reduction Proposals

In addition to the fiscal commission discussed above, the FY20 11 President's Budget also includes other deficit reduction measures, including a freeze in non-security discretionary spending over the next three fiscal years, a fee imposed on the financial services industry over at least the next 10 years to cover the cost of TARP, and other tax proposals aimed at increasing revenue.[57] Some of the Administration's tax proposals include closing the "carried interest" loophole, allowing lower tax rates on households earning more than $250,000 to expire, and reforming the taxation of international income. Together, these proposals are aimed at cutting the deficit in half by the end of the President's current term.

Ongoing Economic Recovery and Other Initiatives

As the economy continues to recover, job creation, strengthening the middle class, and providing recovery assistance to rural and urban communities are top Administration priorities to restore economic growth. Education, clean energy, and infrastructure, including major investments in urban and rural communities, are targeted sectors for job creation. The Administration also specifies initiatives to provide assistance to small businesses by ensuring their access to credit and eliminating certain taxes on investments. Other specific research and development funding is also provided in the areas of science, biomedical research, and space exploration.

Funding for various infrastructure and energy initiatives is included as part of the President's job- creation proposals. These initiatives for a new energy economy include investing in a smart, energy-efficient, and reliable electric grid, a clean-energy future, and science research and development funding to address energy independence and climate change. Some funding for these initiatives was also contained in ARRA.

Finally, the President is proposing to increase outlays for education and training with the goal of developing a more skilled and productive labor force. Funding will be provided at both the federal level as well as via grants to state and local governments for individual programs such as Head Start and aid for higher education. Additional outlays for education and training purposes are earmarked for infrastructure investment and research and development. Funding for education-related jobs and an expansion of early childhood education programs was also provided for in ARRA.

Congressional Consideration of the FY2011 Budget Resolution

The House and Senate Budget Committees are responsible for formulating and reporting an annual budget resolution. The budget committees typically develop the budget resolution as they receive information and testimony from various sources, such as the Administration, CBO, and congressional committees with jurisdiction over spending and revenues. The timetable established in the Congressional Budget Act directs the Senate Budget Committee to report a budget resolution by April 1, and for the House and Senate to reach final agreement on a budget resolution by April 15.[58]

On April 22, 2010, the Senate Budget Committee reported the budget resolution (S.Con.Res. 60) by a vote of 12-10. The resolution provided for revenue levels of $1,838 billion and outlays of $3,191 billion in FY20 11 for a deficit of $1,260 billion, or approximately 8.4% of GDP. By FY20 15, the deficit is projected to fall to $545 billion or 3.0% of GDP. The resolution includes a freeze of non-security discretionary spending at the FY20 10 levels between FY20 11 -FY20 13, similar to what was proposed in the President's budget. Spending levels for FY20 11 also include an additional cut of $4 billion to security spending, targeted at international affairs. The Senate budget resolution achieves greater deficit reduction, relative to the President's budget, by requiring offsets for certain tax provisions.

The Senate resolution also contains reconciliation instructions to the Senate Finance Committee, directing them to report legislation within their jurisdiction that would reduce the deficit by $2 billion over the FY20 10 to FY20 15 period. If reported, reconciliation legislation is considered under expedited procedures on the House and Senate floor. The Senate has not taken any further action on the budget resolution.

On July 1, 2010, the House adopted a budget enforcement resolution (H.Res. 1493), which established a top line discretionary spending level for FY20 11 for House appropriators of $1,314 billion. The measure also contained other budget enforcement provisions.

Considerations for Congress

Congress faces ongoing budgetary challenges in FY20 11 with both short-run and long-run budget priorities that may conflict in critical ways. In the short term, economic issues may dominate policy debates, creating pressure for higher deficit spending. In the long term, increasing federal health care costs are expected to keep mandatory spending rising.

Short-Term Considerations

Although economic growth returned in the third and fourth quarters of 2009, signaling a possible end to the economic recession, conditions remain weak due to budget challenges facing state and local governments, high levels of consumer debt, and continuing weakness in many real estate markets. Most economists expect unemployment rates to remain elevated for the medium term. As discussed above, Congress may choose to enact more stimulus in response to the state of the economy, which may add to the budget deficit in FY20 11 and beyond.

General Budget Issues

Congress may wish to consider some general budgeting issues beyond these short term considerations.

CBO Budget Documents

The Congressional Budget Office (CBO) provides data and analysis to Congress throughout the budget and appropriations process. Each January, CBO issues a *Budget and Economic Outlook* that contains current-law baseline estimates of outlays and revenues. In March, CBO typically issues an analysis of the President's budget submission with revised baseline estimates and projections. In late summer, CBO issues an updated *Budget and Economic Outlook* with new baseline projections.

In these documents, CBO sets a current-law baseline as a benchmark to evaluate whether legislative proposals would increase or decrease outlays and revenue collection. Baseline estimates are not intended to predict likely future outcomes, but to show what spending and revenues would be if current law remained in effect. CBO typically evaluates the budgetary consequences of legislative proposals and the Joint Committee on Taxation (JCT) evaluates the consequences of revenue proposals.

CBO also releases other periodic publications focusing on the future fiscal health of the United States. In their publication, *The Long-Term Budget Outlook*, CBO makes projections on the state of the federal budget to FY2083. They discuss spending and revenue levels and the related issues that they expect will arise under different policy assumptions. In their *Budget Options* volumes, they provide specific policy options and the impact they will have on spending and revenues over a 10-year budget window. They also provide arguments for and against enacting each policy.

Budget Transparency

The budget, reflecting the size and complexity of the federal government, is complicated and detailed. The budget books that OMB compiles provide an enormous amount of information, and other budget data reported by federal agencies provide even more detail on federal spending plans. The Federal Funding Accountability and Transparency Act of 2006 (P.L. 109-282) included several measures to increase the accessibility of budget information. For example, as a result of that act, OMB now runs the USAspending.gov website, which provides detailed information on federal spending. Some, however, have raised concerns about the quality of those data.[59] Moreover, it is not clear that those data are thoroughly coordinated with other federal budgeting data systems.

Congress and the President have undertaken additional efforts in an attempt to improve transparency in light of the large amounts of spending currently occurring as a result of economic stabilization efforts and federal financial interventions. Websites, such as Recovery.gov, were launched to track stimulus spending. The Congressional Oversight Panel was established in the Emergency Economic Stabilization Act to oversee TARP spending. Despite this, criticisms remain and requests for greater transparency continue.

In certain cases, despite the large amount of data provided by OMB and other government agencies, it can be difficult to answer relatively simple budget questions. Critics maintain that the federal government in general and OMB in particular should take steps to make data on federal spending even more transparent to taxpayers and more useful to policymakers. Even as the President's budget mentions "a new tracking tool" to provide daily updates on spending by agency, Congress wants to consider requiring these changes to provide more organized and transparent budget data to citizens and to itself. [60]

Budget Enforcement Measures

The Budget Enforcement Act and other budget enforcement legislation was widely credited for laying the groundwork for the federal government's surpluses between FY1998-FY2001. One of the components of this group of legislation, statutory PAYGO, which effectively was terminated in December 2002, discouraged the enactment of new mandatory spending and revenue legislation that is not deficit neutral (i.e., legislation that would cause, or increase, a deficit or reduce a surplus) due to the threat of sequestration.[61] President Obama's budget included various proposals for budget process reform; perhaps the most significant proposal from the perspective of budget enforcement was a proposal to reinstate statutory PAYGO procedures.[62] In February 2010, the House and Senate once again enacted statutory PAYGO, similar to what was in effect in the 1 990s and early 2000s (Title I of P.L. 111-139). While PAYGO procedures do not facilitate reducing existing deficit levels, they may help to keep deficit levels from increasing due to legislative action. Critics note, however, that the new statutory PAYGO procedures allow for the enactment of legislation in several "current policy" areas that could boost deficit levels significantly. [63]

Long-Term Considerations

Annual budget deficits or surpluses are not always the best indication of long-term fiscal stability. Most economists agree that, under certain conditions, running a budget deficit may be necessary to provide economic stimulus or pull an economy out of recession. A large budget deficit in a single year, in itself, does not necessarily indicate a longer-term problem. The federal government, however, faces serious long-term budget challenges. Some measures of fiscal solvency in the long term indicate that, under current policy, the U.S. may face a major future crisis, specifically as it relates to rising health care costs and the likely impact on government- financed health care spending.

CBO, GAO, and the Administration agree that the current mix of federal fiscal policies is unsustainable in the long term. The nation's aging population, combined with rising health care costs per beneficiary, seems likely to keep federal health costs rising faster than per capita GDP. CBO projected in June 2010 that under current policy, federal spending on Medicare and Medicaid would grow from 5.5% of GDP today to about 10% of GDP in 2035, and to more than 17% by 2080.[64] The 2010 Economic Report of the President also called the trajectory of future federal spending on Medicare and Medicaid unsustainable.[65] GAO's recent long-term fiscal simulations, under an alternative policy scenario, projected debt held by the public as a share of GDP to exceed the post World War II historical high in about 10 years.[66]

Keeping future federal outlays at 20% of GDP, approximately its current share, and leaving fiscal policies unchanged, according to CBO projections, would require drastic reductions in all spending other than that for Medicare, Social Security, and Medicaid, or reigning in the costs of these programs. Under the extension of current policy, CBO estimates that the nation's current fiscal gap, a present-value measure of fiscal imbalance for a given time period, would reach 0.7% of GDP over the next 75 years. This means that an immediate and permanent reduction in spending, increase in revenues, or a combination of spending cuts and revenue increases amounting to 0.7% of GDP would be needed to make the government's debt the same size (relative to the size of the economy) at the end of that period as it was at the beginning. Under an alternative fiscal scenario, which incorporates some policy changes that are widely expected to occur and that policymakers have regularly made in the past, the fiscal gap reaches 8.7% of GDP.[67] This indicates that an immediate and permanent reduction in spending, increase in revenues, or a combination of spending cuts and revenue increases amounting to 8.7% of GDP would be needed to make the government's debt the same size (relative to the size of the economy) at the end of that period as it was at the beginning.[68] Enacting policies to close the fiscal gap under either scenario would likely require significant changes in major entitlement programs as these programs are projected to be responsible for the majority of the long-term growth in federal spending.[69]

As the economic recovery continues, Congress may focus more effort on balancing the budget and reining in the debt. This would require less spending, increases in revenue collections, fasterthan-average economic growth, or a combination of these things. Many economists agree that having some federal debt is a good thing because it builds credit which allows for more favorable borrowing terms. It encourages investment within the country because federal debt is seen as relatively low-risk and safe. Debt is not free, however, and requires interest payments that can strain budgets if debt levels and interest rates are high. High debt levels could limit the government's flexibility in meeting its obligations or in responding to emerging needs of its citizens. Ultimately, failing to take action to reduce the projected growth in the debt potentially might lead to future insolvency or government default.[70]

End Notes

[1] For more information, see CRS Report 98-721, *Introduction to the Federal Budget Process*, by Robert Keith.

[2] U.S. Department of Commerce, Bureau of Economic Analysis, "Gross Domestic Product: Fourth Quarter 2009 (Advanced Estimate)," press release BEA 10-02, January 29, 2010, available at http://www.bea.gov/newsreleases/ national/gdp/2010/txt/gdp4q09_adv.txt.

[3] CRS Report 98-325, *The Federal Fiscal Year*, by Bill Heniff Jr.

[4] The contents of the Presidential budget submission are governed by U.S. Code, Title 31, Sec. 1105.

[5] U.S. Congressional Budget Office, *Historical Tables*, available at *http://www.cbo.gov/ budget/historical.shtml.*

[6] Most economists use data on federal outlays to track larger budget trends, while most program analysts use budget authority to track changes in specific program areas.

[7] For further explanation of the changing costs of these programs, see the section of this chapter titled, "Changing Budgetary Impact of Major Financial Interventions and Economic Recovery Programs."

[8] Currently, the Social Security program collects more through the payroll tax than is needed to pay out current benefits, thus generating a surplus in the Social Security Trust Fund. By law, surplus dollars are required to be invested in non-marketable Treasury securities. From an overall budget perspective, these surpluses are used to offset other federal spending, thereby decreasing the current budget deficit while increasing the amount of Treasury securities held in the Trust Fund.

[9] For more information on trends in discretionary and mandatory spending, see CRS Report RL34424, *Trends in Discretionary Spending*, by D. Andrew Austin and Mindy R. Levit and

CRS Report RL33074, *Mandatory Spending Since 1962*, by D. Andrew Austin and Mindy R. Levit.

[10] For more information see CRS Report RS20129, *Entitlements and Appropriated Entitlements in the Federal Budget Process*, by Bill Heniff Jr.

[11] Mandatory spending is controlled by established parameters for government commitments in permanent law, such as Social Security benefit levels and eligibility requirements. Once these laws have been established, mandatory funding for most programs must be included in annual appropriations bills as the appropriations committees must provide the budget authority needed to meet the commitment. Unlike discretionary spending, changes to mandatory funding levels can only be made through changes in the authorizing legislation.

[12] The assumption that discretionary spending will remain constant in real terms is at odds with the historical growth rate of discretionary spending, leading to projections which often understate discretionary spending levels. For more information, see the section titled "Budget Baseline Projections" later in this chapter.

[13] U.S. Congressional Budget Office, *Historical Tables*, available at *http://www.cbo.gov/budget/historical.shtml.*

[14] In various reports, the Congressional Budget Office, the Government Accountability Office, and the Administration agree that the federal government's budget is on an unsustainable path. For more information, see the section of this chapter titled, "Long-Term Considerations."

[15] U.S. Congressional Budget Office, *Historical Tables*, available at *http://www.cbo.gov/budget/historical.shtml.*

[16] For more information, see CRS Report RL34425, *Expiration and Extension of the Individual Income Tax Cuts Enacted in 2001 Through 2008*, by Maxim Shvedov and CRS Report R40414, *Tax Reform: An Overview of Proposals in the 111th Congress*, by James M. Bickley.

[17] See CRS Report RL33623, *Long-Term Measures of Fiscal Imbalance*, by D. Andrew Austin.

[18] Committee for a Responsible Federal Budget, *Good Deficit / Bad Deficit*, April 2009.

[19] U.S. Office of Management and Budget, *Budget for Fiscal Year 2011, Historical Tables*, Table 1-3, available at http://www.whitehouse.gov/omb/budget/fy2011/assets

[20] Gross federal debt is also referred to as total debt or total public debt outstanding. Intragovernmental debt is also referred to as intragovernmental holdings or debt held by federal government accounts.

[21] U.S. Office of Management and Budget, *Budget of the U.S. Government, Fiscal Year 2009, Analytical Perspectives*, Feb. 2008, p. 408.

[22] In FY2009, the increase in the deficit was larger than that of debt held by the public due to the nature of the obligations incurred as a result of the government conservatorship of Fannie Mae and Freddie Mac and the TARP program. For a larger discussion of why this occurred, see the section titled "Changing Budgetary Impact of Major Financial Interventions and Economic Recovery Programs" later in this chapter.

[23] For more information, see CRS Report RL34712, *Ebbs and Flows of Federal Debt*, by Mindy R. Levit.

[24] General Accountability Office, *Debt Ceiling: Analysis of Actions Taken During the 2003 Debt Issuance Suspension Period*, GAO-04-526, May 20, 2004.

[25] U.S. Congressional Budget Office, *The Budget and Economic Outlook: Fiscal Years 2010 to 2020*, Tables D-2, available at http://www.cbo.gov/ftpdocs/108xx/doc10871/01-26-Outlook.pdf.

[26] For further details, see CRS Report RL3 1967, *The Debt Limit: History and Recent Increases*, by D. Andrew Austin and Mindy R. Levit.

[27] U.S. Congressional Budget Office, *Historical Tables*, Tables F-5 and F-6, available at http://www.cbo.gov/budget/ historical.shtml.

[28] Carmen M. Reinhart and Kenneth S. Rogoff, "The Aftermath of Financial Crises," *American Economic Review*, vol. 99 (2009), no. 2; Alan Auerbach and William Gale, "The Economic

Crisis and the Fiscal Crisis: 2009 and Beyond," Tax Policy Center working paper, February 2009, available at http://www.taxpolicycenter.org/UploadedPDF/411 843_economic_crisis.pdf.

[29] The original cost estimate for ARRA was increased by $75 billion due to revised estimates of outlays for income security programs (unemployment insurance and SNAP program) and a higher participation rates in the Build America Bonds program. U.S. Congressional Budget Office, *The Budget and Economic Outlook: Fiscal Years 2010 to 2020*, January 2010, Appendix A, available at http://www.cbo.gov/ftpdocs/108xx/doc10871/01-26-Outlook.pdf.

[30] For more information on the provisions of ARRA, see CRS Report R40537, *American Recovery and Reinvestment Act of 2009 (P.L. 111-5): Summary and Legislative History*, by Clinton T. Brass et al.

[31] For further details on these actions, see CRS Report R41073, *Government Interventions in Response to Financial Turmoil*, by Baird Webel and Marc Labonte.

[32] For more information, see CRS Report R41350, *The Dodd-Frank Wall Street Reform and Consumer Protection Act: Issues and Summary*, coordinated by Baird Webel.

[33] U.S. Congressional Budget Office, H.R. 4173, Dodd-Frank Wall Street Reform and Consumer Protection Act, June 29, 2010, available at *http://www.cbo.gov/ftpdocs/116xx/doc11601/hr4173amendment.pdf.*

[34] The budgetary impact of the Economic Stimulus Act of 2008 was different from ARRA's in that it was comparatively small and was composed, in large part, of stimulus checks sent to taxpayers. Because rebate checks were dispersed relatively quickly, the impact on the deficit from this legislation was largely incurred in FY2008.

[35] Mandated by Section 123 of the Emergency Economic Stabilization Act (P.L. 110-343).

[36] U.S. Congressional Budget Office, *Report on the Troubled Asset Relief Program—March 2010*, March 2010, Table 1, available at http://www.cbo.gov/ftpdocs/112xx/doc11227/03-17-TARP.pdf.

[37] U.S Treasury, *Troubled Assets Relief Program Monthly 105(a) Report*—September 2009, October 9, 2009, p. 3, available at http://financialstability.gov/latest/reportsanddocs.html.

[38] U.S. Congressional Budget Office, *The Budget and Economic Outlook: Fiscal Years 2010 to 2020*, January 2010, Table 1-7.

[39] For more information on these accounting methodologies, see U.S. Congressional Budget Office, *CBO's Budgetary Treatment of Fannie Mae and Freddie Mac*, January 2010, available at http://www.cbo.gov/ftpdocs/108xx/doc10878/ 01-13-FannieFreddie.pdf and U.S. Office of Management and Budget, *The Budget for Fiscal Year 2011*, *Analytical Perspectives*, pp. 346-358, available at *http://www.whitehouse.gov/omb/budget/fy2011/assets*

[40] U.S. Congressional Budget Office, *An Analysis of the President's Budgetary Proposals for Fiscal Year 2011*, March 2010, Table 1-1.

[41] U.S. Office of Management and Budget, *Budget for Fiscal Year 2011*, *The Budget*, Tables S-2 and S-7.

[42] U.S. Office of Management and Budget, *Budget for Fiscal Year 2011*, *Mid-Session Review*, Table 1 and pp. 4-5.

[43] For more information and a comprehensive list of CRS reports on this issue, see "Comprehensive Descriptions of the Patient Protection and Affordable Care Act" at http://www.crs.gov/Pages/subissue.aspx?cliid=3746&parentid=13.

[44] Of the total budget deficit impact over the FY2010-FY2019 period, $124 billion in net reductions derives from the health care and revenue provisions, while the remaining $19 billion in net reductions derives from the education provisions contained in HCERA. U.S. Congressional Budget Office, H.R. 4872, Reconciliation Act of 2010 (Final Health Care Legislation), March 20, 2010, available at http://www.cbo.gov/ftpdocs/113xx/doc11379/ AmendReconProp.pdf.

[45] U.S. Office of Management and Budget, *Budget for Fiscal Year 2011*, *The Budget*, p. 11.

[46] For more information, see CRS Report RL33 110, *The Cost of Iraq, Afghanistan, and Other Global War on Terror Operations Since 9/11*, by Amy Belasco.

[47] For more information, see CRS Report R41232, *FY2010 Supplemental for Wars, Disaster Assistance, Haiti Relief, and Other Programs*, coordinated by Amy Belasco.

[48] For more information, see CRS Report R41053, *Jobs for Main Street Act: Education, Training and Direct Assistance Provisions*, coordinated by Karen Spar.

[49] U.S. Congressional Budget Office, CBO Estimate of the Statutory Pay-As-You-Go Effects for an Amendment to the Senate Amendment to the House Amendment to the Senate Amendment to H.R. 2847, March 4, 2010, available at *http://www.cbo.gov/ftpdo cs/112xx/doc11275/hr2847HPaygo.pdf.*

[50] For more information, see CRS Report RL33362, *Unemployment Insurance: Available Unemployment Benefits and Legislative Activity*, by Katelin P. Isaacs, Julie M. Whittaker, and Alison M. Shelton and CRS Report R40907, *Medicare Physician Payment Updates and the Sustainable Growth Rate (SGR) System*, by Jim Hahn.

[51] While some budget enforcement legislation constraining the computation of CBO baseline estimates has expired, CBO has continued to follow those legislative guidelines.

[52] The President's budget proposals can be found on the OMB website at *http://www.whitehou se.gov/omb/budget/*. The Supplemental Materials include the Federal Credit Supplement, the Object Class Analysis, the Balances of Budget Authority, and the Public Budget Database.

[53] For details of these projections, see U.S. Office of Management and Budget, *Budget for Fiscal Year 2011, The Budget*, Tables S-1 (Proposed Budget) and S-7 (BEA Baseline and Current Policy).

[54] The tax cuts were enacted in the Economic Growth and Taxpayer Relief Act of 2001 (EGTRRA; P.L. 107-16) and the Jobs and Growth Tax Relief Reconciliation Act of 2003 (JGTRRA; P.L. 108-27).

[55] U.S. Office of Management and Budget, *Budget for Fiscal Year 2011, The Budget*, Tables S-1.

[56] President of the United States, *Executive Order 13531—National Commission on Fiscal Responsibility and Reform*, February 1 8, 20 1 0, available at *http://www.whitehouse.gov /the-press-office/executive-order-national-commissionfiscal-responsibility-and-reform*. See also http://www.fiscalcommission.gov/.

[57] For more information on the President's proposal to freeze non-security discretionary spending, see CRS Report R41 174, *Impact on the Federal Budget of Freezing Non-Security Discretionary Spending*, by Mindy R. Levit.

[58] For more information on the congressional budget process, see CRS Report RS20368, *Overview of the Congressional Budget Process*, by Bill Heniff Jr.

[59] For more information, see CRS Report RL3471 8, *The Federal Funding Accountability and Transparency Act: Implementation and Proposed Amendments*, by Garrett Hatch.

[60] U.S. Office of Management and Budget, *Budget for Fiscal Year 2011, The Budget*, p. 44.

[61] See CRS Report RL34300, *Pay-As-You-Go Procedures for Budget Enforcement*, by Robert Keith.

[62] Office of Management and Budget, *Budget of the United States Government, Fiscal Year 2011, Analytical Perspectives*, Feb. 1, 2009 (see Chapter 13, "Budget Process," pp. 143-155).

[63] The PAYGO legislation enacted by the House and Senate exempts the extension of certain spending and revenue measures, including a five-year fix to scheduled cuts to Medicare physician reimbursement rates, a two-year fix to prevent the Alternative Minimum Tax from hitting more taxpayers and to restore the Estate Tax to 2009 rates and exemptions, and a permanent extension of middle-class tax cuts.

[64] U.S. Congressional Budget Office, *The Long-Term Budget Outlook*, June 2010, p. 7 and "Supplemental Material."

[65] Council of Economic Advisors, *Economic Report of the President*, February 2010, pp.140.

[66] Government Accountability Office, *The Federal Government's Long-Term Fiscal Outlook: Fall 2009 Update* (GAO10-137SP), October 15, 2009, pp.1.

[67] The alternative fiscal scenario includes things like the extension of certain expiring tax provisions, the continued indexation of AMT to inflation, and Medicare physician payment rates growing with the Medicare economic index. For a complete description of the assumptions included in the extended baseline and alternative fiscal scenarios, see U.S. Congressional Budget Office, *The Long-Term Budget Outlook*, June 2010, Table 1-1.

[68] U.S. Congressional Budget Office, *The Long-Term Budget Outlook*, June 2010, Table 1-3.

[69] U.S. Congressional Budget Office, *The Long-Term Budget Outlook*, June 2010, p. 8.

[70] Recent trends in the credit default swap market imply an increased, albeit still small, market perception of the likelihood of default on certain Treasury securities. In past years, Treasury securities were typically regarded as risk- free. See Alan Auerbach and William Gale, "The Economic Crisis and the Fiscal Crisis: 2009 and Beyond: An Update," Tax Policy Center working paper, September 2009, available at http://www.brookings.edu/~/media papers/2009/06_fiscal_crisis_gale/06_fiscal_crisis_gale_update.pdf.

In: United States Federal Budget Process ISBN: 978-1-61209-844-9
Editors: Gerard T. Brenner, et al.

Chapter 9

FY2011 BUDGET PROPOSALS AND PROJECTIONS

D. Andrew Austin

SUMMARY

This chapter provides an overview of major budget estimates and projections for the FY2011 federal budget cycle. The report presents and compares budget projections calculated by the Obama Administration's Office of Management and Budget (OMB) and the Congressional Budget Office (CBO). In addition, the report discusses major budgetary issues.

The congressional budget process usually begins once the Administration submits its budget to Congress. The Senate Budget Committee passed a version of a budget resolution (S.Con.Res. 60) in April, and the House adopted a deeming resolution (H.Res. 1500; H.Res. 1493) in July.

The current economic climate continues to pose major challenges to policymakers shaping the FY2011 federal budget. Although the economy has shown some signs of recovery from an economic recession that many economists consider the most severe since the Great Depression, unemployment remains at high levels. While the U.S. economy grew at an annual rate of 5.0% in the last quarter of 2009 in inflation-adjusted terms, after falling sharply in the last quarter of 2008 and the first quarter of 2009, annualized growth was 3.7% in the first quarter of 2010 and 1.6% in the second quarter. The national unemployment rate stood at 9.5% in July 2010 and is projected to decline slowly. Weakness in residential and commercial real estate, high household debt levels, and fiscal challenges facing state and local governments may contribute to a long and slow economic recovery. The recession and the prospect of a slow recovery have strongly affected budget estimates and projections. OMB issued updated budget projections in July 2010, and CBO issued a budget baseline update in August 2010.

Federal spending tied to means-tested social programs has risen due to rising unemployment, while federal revenues are falling as individuals' incomes drop and corporate profits sink. Federal revenues fell 17% between FY2007 and FY2009. Estimated costs of federal interventions in financial markets have fallen since late 2008 and early 2009, although fiscal risks associated with mortgage giants Fannie Mae and Freddie Mac remain. Federal deficits, according to OMB and CBO projections, will likely remain high relative to historic norms over the next few years. Long- run fiscal challenges have received renewed attention as the ratio of federal debt held by the public to GDP, which compares the accumulation of federal debt (excluding intragovernmental debt) to the size of the economy as a whole, reached 53% at the end of FY2009 and, according to OMB and CBO estimates, will exceed 60% at the end of FY2010

The Obama Administration released its FY20 11 budget proposals on February 1, 2010. The Administration featured policy initiatives targeted at speeding up economic recovery, reducing the unemployment rate, implementing health insurance reform, overhauling financial regulation, and stabilizing housing markets and the automobile industry. The Administration also proposed a three-year freeze in non-security discretionary spending, which currently comprises about 15% of total federal outlays. The Administration's *Mid Session Review*, released on July 23, 2010, estimated that FY20 10 revenues would be $33 billion lower, outlays would be $118 billion lower, and deficits would be $84 billion lower than estimates issued in February. CBO issued updated estimates on August 19, 2010.

The federal budget outlines spending levels for government programs and how that spending will be funded, reflecting the policy priorities of Congress and the President. This chapter provides an overview of major budget estimates and projections for the FY2011 federal budget cycle. The report presents and compares budget projections calculated by the Obama Administration's Office of Management and Budget (OMB) and the Congressional Budget Office (CBO). In addition, the report discusses selected major budgetary issues.

Overview of the FY2011 Budget Cycle

The congressional budget process, which includes the annual budget resolution and appropriations bills, usually begins once the Administration submits its budget to Congress.[1] As Congress deliberates over the budget, the Administration often revises its proposals as it interacts with Members of Congress and as national and international economic conditions change.[2]

Economic Conditions Present Continuing Budget Challenges

The economy continues to post major challenges to policymakers shaping the FY2011 federal budget. The economic recession, which many economists consider the most severe American recession since the Great Depression, has strongly affected budget estimates and projections. The U.S. economy shrank at an annual real (i.e., inflation-adjusted) rate of 6.8% in the last quarter of 2008, the biggest fall since 1982, followed by a 4.9% fall in annual-rate terms in the first quarter of 2009. While real GDP grew at an estimated annual rate of 5.0% in the fourth quarter of 2009, perhaps signaling the end of the recession, growth in 2010 has been slow relative to many other economic recoveries.[3] Estimates put real annualized growth in the first quarter of 2010 at 3.7% and only 1.6% for the second quarter.[4] While financial markets by mid-2009 have stabilized significantly, the chairman of the Federal Reserve Board recently described the state of the economy as "unusually uncertain."[5] While the economy is showing some signs of recovery, the national unemployment rate, which was 9.5% in July 2010, is projected to decline slowly.[6] CBO estimates that the national unemployment rate will not recede to the 5% level until 2014.[7] Some economists have become increasingly worried about the possibility of a "double-dip" recession, which would complicate existing budgetary challenges, although many forecasters do not predict a "double-dip."

Federal spending tied to means-tested social programs has risen due to elevated levels of unemployment, while federal revenues are projected to fall as individuals' incomes drop and corporate profits sink. Total federal revenues fell 17% between FY2007 and FY2009, and corporate income tax receipts fell even more sharply. CBO estimated in August 2010 that federal revenues will stabilize in FY2010, increasing from $2,105 billion in FY2009 (14.8% of GDP) to $2,143 billion in FY2010 (14.6% of GDP), and are projected to rebound somewhat in FY2011 to $2,648 billion (17.5% of GDP).[8] Federal deficits, however, will likely be high relative to historic norms in FY2011, according to OMB and CBO projections. While federal deficits, according to CBO current-law baseline projections, will fall to 2.5% of GDP in FY2014, many budget experts consider the baseline assumptions, which were set in budget enforcement legislation, overly optimistic (see discussion in next section for details). In the later years of the current 10-year baseline budget window, federal deficits are projected to rebound, in large part due to the retirement of baby boomers and rising health care costs.

The federal government responded to the economic slowdown with an array of policy responses unprecedented in recent decades, including fiscal stimulus in the form of new spending and tax cuts. The federal government and the Federal Reserve also expanded or initiated major loan programs. As the economy recovers, the federal government and Federal Reserve plan to shrink or discontinue those programs as financial markets return to a more normal state. Some federal interventions, such as the Troubled Assets Relief Program, are now expected to cost far less than previous estimates, but the federal government may still face substantial credit risks associated with the takeovers of AIG, Fannie Mae, Freddie Mac, and large holdings in automobile manufacturers. Furthermore, the federal government could face new fiscal challenges if economic recovery falters or if financial turmoil reemerges.

FY2011 Budget Submission

The Obama Administration released its FY2011 budget submission on February 1, 2010.[9] The Administration featured policy initiatives targeted at speeding up economic recovery, reducing the unemployment rate, enacting health insurance reform, overhauling financial regulation, and stabilizing housing markets and the automobile industry. The *Mid Session Review* was released on July 23, 2010.

On February 18, 2010, President Obama set up the National Commission on Fiscal Responsibility and Reform, which was charged with finding ways to "improve the fiscal situation in the medium term and to achieve fiscal sustainability over the long run."[10] The commission is slated to issue a report on December 1.

On April 22, the Senate Budget Committee passed its FY20 11 budget resolution (S.Con.Res. 60). As of the date of this chapter, however, neither the House nor the Senate had agreed to a budget resolution. On July 1, 2010, the

House, by adopting H.Res. 1500, was considered to have agreed to a "deeming" resolution (H.Res. 1493), which serves some of the purposes of a budget resolution. In particular, deeming resolutions provide a basis for ongoing budget enforcement.[11]

BUDGET ESTIMATES, PROPOSALS, AND PROJECTIONS

Table 1 contains budget estimates for FY2011 from CBO and the Administration (the Office of Management and Budget, OMB). House and Senate Budget Committees are expected to issue their own budget totals in a budget resolution that reflects congressional funding priorities.

Budget estimates and projections vary due to differing underlying economic, technical, and budget-estimating assumptions and techniques, as well as differences in policy assumptions. Minor differences in underlying assumptions, which may generate small short-term discrepancies, can produce wide divergences in projected long-term budget paths. In addition, the extraordinary nature of federal responses to financial turmoil and economic recession have complicated some scoring issues. Budget estimates issued by the President, CBO, or by others, should be expected to change as new data arrive or as economic conditions change.

CBO current-law baseline projections are computed using assumptions set forth in budget enforcement legislation. The CBO baseline projections are not intended to serve as a prediction of what budget outcomes are most plausible or likely. Rather, the CBO baseline projections are designed to serve as a budgeting tool, which is used to determine how legislative changes would increase or decrease the federal deficit.[12]

CBO baseline projections typically yield estimates of higher growth in revenue and slower growth of discretionary spending relative to scenarios that independent forecasters consider likely. CBO baseline projections presume that

- discretionary spending remains constant in inflation-adjusted terms;
- the 2001 and 2003 tax cuts expire after FY20 10 (as current law specifies);[13]
- the existing "patch" to the alternative minimum tax (AMT), which currently applies to tax year 2009, would lapse;[14]
- emergency unemployment benefits will not be extended;[15] and

- cuts scheduled for Medicare physician services (Part B) as a result of "sustainable growth rate" calculations will not be delayed or cancelled. [16]

After FY2010, according to baseline projections, the expiration of most of the tax cuts from 2001 and 2003 would increase federal receipts. The assumption that these tax cuts expire and that growth in discretionary spending is zero in real terms explains much of the declining deficits that emerge over the 10-year CBO baseline forecast window and in the OMB BEA (Budget Enforcement Act) baseline. The Joint Committee on Taxation estimates that

- indexing the AMT to inflation for FY20 1 0-FY2020 would cost $584 billion and
- extending tax cuts enacted in 2001 and 2003 (mainly EGTRRA and JGTRRA) would cost $2,465 billion over the FY20 11 -FY2020 period. [17]

Beyond the end of the current 10-year forecast window, federal deficits are expected to grow rapidly, largely because of growing health care costs and the retirement of the baby boomers, unless major policy changes are made.[18]

CBO's first budget report for the FY2011 budget cycle, released in January 2010, contained current-law budget baseline and economic projections for FY2011 through FY2020.[19] This CBO report projected a FY2011 current-law baseline total deficit of $980 billion, significantly smaller than the estimated FY2009 ($1,414 billion) and FY2010 ($1,349) deficits, but far larger than the FY2008 deficit ($459 billion).

CBO's January report also included estimated budgetary effects of selected policies on revenues and outlays. Those projections, which are based on assumptions that differ from current-law baseline conventions, can be used to assess costs of alternative policies.[20] These alternative policy proposals interact in important ways, so that the costs of enacting two of these proposals may differ significantly from the sum of the costs of implementing each proposal separately. In particular, the effects of indexing the AMT and the extension of the 2001 and 2003 tax cuts interact in significant ways.

Table 1. Budget Estimates and Proposals for FY2011

	Revenues	Outlays	Discretionary Outlays	Mandatory Outlays	Deficits			Debt Held by the Public
					Total	On-Budget	Off-Budget	
Billions of Current Dollars								
CBO Baseline, 1/2010	2,670	3,650	1,371	2,045	-980	-1,076	96	9,785
President's FY20 11 Budget, 2/09	2,567	3,834	1,415	2,165	- 1,267	-1,363	96	10,498
OMB FY20 1 1 Current Policy Baseline, 2/2010	2,583	3,728	1,376	2,100	- 1,145	-1,241	96	
OMB FY20 1 1 BEA Baseline, 2/2010	2,782	3,694	1,396	2,050	-912	-1,008	96	
Prelim CBO Est. of Pres. Budget 3/2010	2,461	3,802	1,401	2,157	- 1,341	-1,435	93	10,510
CBO Est. of Pres. Budget 3/24/2010	2,460	3,802	1,401	2,156	- 1,342	-1,435	93	10,512
CBO Rev. Baseline 3/20 10	2,673	3,668	1,373	2,058	-995	-1,089	94	9,853
CBO Rev. Baseline 3/24/2010	2,673	3,668	1,373	2,058	-996	-1,089	94	9,862
Budget Resolution - S Budget 4/2010	2,511	3,770	1,413	2,116	- 1,260	-1,353	93	10,173
President's FY20 1 1 Budget, MSR 7/20 10	2,426	3,842	1,433	2,186	- 1,416	-1,495	79	10,550
OMB FY201 1 Current Policy Baseline, 7/2010	2,478	3,711	1,394	2,094	- 1,233	-1,312	79	

Table 1 (Continued)

	Revenues	Outlays	Discretionary Outlays	Mandatory Outlays	Deficits			Debt Held by the Public
					Total	On-Budget	Off-Budget	
OMB FY20 1 1 BEA Baseline, 7/20 10	2,682	3,694	1,419	2,055	-1,012	-1,091	79	
CBO Rev. Baseline 8/20 10	2,648	3,714	1,404	2,085	-1,066	-1,154	88	10,007
As % GDP								
CBO Baseline, 1/2010	17.8%	24.3%	9.1%	13.6%	-6.5%	-7.2%	0.6%	65.3%
President's FY20 11 Budget, 2/09	16.8%	25.1%	9.2%	14.2%	-8.3%	-8.9%	0.6%	68.6%
OMB FY201 1 Current Policy Baseline, 2/2010	16.9%	24.4%	9.0%	13.7%	-8.3%	-8.1%	0.6%	
OMB FY201 1 BEA Baseline, 2/2010	18.2%	24.1%	9.1%	13.4%	-8.3%	-6.6%	0.6%	
Prelim CBO Est. of Pres. Budget 3/2010	16.4%	25.4%	9.3%	14.4%	-8.9%	-9.6%	0.6%	68.7%
CBO Est. of Pres. Budget 3/24/2010	16.4%	25.4%	9.3%	14.4%	-8.9%	-9.6%	0.6%	70.1%
CBO Rev. Baseline 3/2010	17.8%	24.5%	9.2%	13.7%	-6.6%	-7.3%	0.6%	65.7%
CBO Rev. Baseline 3/24/2010	17.8%	24.5%	9.2%	13.7%	-6.6%	-7.3%	0.6%	65.8%
Budget Resolution - S Budget 4/2010	16.6%	24.9%	9.5%	14.0%	-8.3%	-9.9%	0.6%	67.9%
President's FY201 1 Budget, MSR 7/2010	16.4%	25.4%	9.3%	14.4%	-9.3%	-8.9%	0.5%	69.6%

Table 1 (Continued)

	Revenues	Outlays	Discretionary Outlays	Mandatory Outlays	Deficits			Debt Held by the Public
					Total	On-Budget	Off-Budget	
OMB FY201 1 Current Policy Baseline, 7/2010	17.7%	24.5%	9.2%	13.8%	-8.1%	-8.7%	0.5%	
OMB FY201 1 BEA Baseline, 7/2010	17.5%	24.4%	9.4%	13.6%	-6.7%	-7.2%	0.5%	
CBO Rev. Baseline 8/2010	17.5%	24.5%	9.3%	13.8%	-7.0%	-7.6%	0.6%	66.1%

Sources: CBO and OMB

Notes: CBO estimates of FY20 10 on- and off-budget deficits from January 2010 baseline. Debt held by public is amount projected for September 30, 2011, the end of FY20 11. See text and source documents for additional caveats. "CBO Rev. Baseline 3/2010" data are taken from March 5, 2010, preliminary analysis.

Table 2. Federal Revenues Estimates and Projections for the FY2011 budget: Billions of Current Dollars and as % of GDP

Revenues	FY 2006	FY 2007	FY 2008	FY 2009	FY 2010	FY 2011	FY 2012	FY 2013	FY 2014	FY 2015	FY 2016	FY 2017	FY 2018	FY 2019	FY 2020
Historical	2,407	2,568	2,524	2,105											
CBO Baseline, 1/20 10					2,175	2,670	2,964	3,218	3,465	3,625	3,814	3,996	4,170	4,352	4,563
President's FY20 11 Budget, 2/09					2,165	2,567	2,926	3,188	3,455	3,634	3,887	4,094	4,299	4,507	4,710
OMB FY20 1 1 Current Policy Baseline, 2/2010					2,213	2,583	2,829	3,033	3,269	3,417	3,648	3,838	4,026	4,215	4,400
OMB FY20 1 1 BEA Baseline, 2/2010					2,231	2,782	3,069	3,308	3,581	3,760	4,018	4,235	4,452	4,671	4,885

Table 2 (Continued)

Revenues	FY 2006	FY 2007	FY 2008	FY 2009	FY 2010	FY 2011	FY 2012	FY 2013	FY 2014	FY 2015	FY 2016	FY 2017	FY 2018	FY 2019	FY 2020
Prelim CBO Est. of Pres. Budget 3/2010					2,118	2,461	2,807	3,095	3,341	3,504	3,693	3,869	4,031	4,212	4,417
CBO Est. of Pres. Budget 3/24/20 10					2,118	2,460	2,808	3,095	3,341	3,504	3,693	3,869	4,036	4,211	4,416
CBO Rev. Baseline 3/2010					2,177	2,673	2,967	3,221	3,469	3,629	3,818	4,000	4,174	4,355	4,567
CBO Rev. Baseline 3/24/2010					2,176	2,673	2,967	3,221	3,469	3,629	3,818	4,000	4,174	4,355	4,567
Budget Resolution - S Budget 4/2010					2,152	2,511	2,734	3,131	3,385	3,583	—	—	—	—	—
President's FY2011 Budget, MSR 7/2010					2,132	2,426	2,814	3,102	3,441	3,597	3,853	4,083	4,301	4,523	4,725
OMB FY20 1 1 Current Policy Baseline, 7/20 10					2,142	2,478	2,748	2,997	3,320	3,463	3,708	3,929	4,140	4,353	4,546
OMB FY20 1 1 BEA Baseline, 7/2010					2,142	2,682	2,980	3,260	3,613	3,789	4,064	4,313	4,552	4,793	5,015
CBO Rev. Baseline 8/20 10					2,143	2,648	2,953	3,236	3,561	3,743	3,975	4,201	4,421	4,640	4,856
As % GDP															
Historical	18.2%	18.5%	17.5%	14.8%											
CBO Baseline, 1/2010					14.9%	17.8%	18.8%	19.3%	19.7%	19.7%	19.8%	19.9%	20.0%	20.1%	20.2%
President's FY20 11 Budget, 2/09					14.8%	16.8%	18.1%	18.6%	19.0%	18.9%	19.3%	19.4%	19.5%	19.5%	19.6%
OMB FY20 1 1 Current Policy Baseline, 2/2010					15.1%	16.9%	17.5%	17.6%	18.0%	17.8%	18.1%	18.2%	18.2%	18.3%	18.3%
OMB FY20 1 1 BEA Baseline, 2/2010					15.3%	18.2%	18.9%	19.3%	19.7%	19.6%	19.9%	20.0%	20.2%	20.2%	20.3%

Table 2 (Continued)

Revenues	FY 2006	FY 2007	FY 2008	FY 2009	FY 2010	FY 2011	FY 2012	FY 2013	FY 2014	FY 2015	FY 2016	FY 2017	FY 2018	FY 2019	FY 2020
Prelim CBO Est. of Pres. Budget 3/2010					14.5%	16.4%	17.8%	18.6%	19.0%	19.0%	19.2%	19.3%	19.4%	19.4%	19.6%
CBO Est. of Pres. Budget 3/24/20 10					14.5%	16.4%	17.9%	18.6%	19.0%	19.0%	19.2%	19.3%	19.4%	19.4%	19.6%
CBO Rev. Baseline 3/20 10					14.9%	17.8%	18.9%	19.3%	19.7%	19.7%	19.9%	20.0%	20.0%	20.1%	20.3%
CBO Rev. Baseline 3/24/20 10					14.9%	17.8%	18.9%	19.3%	19.7%	19.7%	19.9%	20.0%	20.0%	20.1%	20.3%
Budget Resolution - S Budget 4/2010					14.7%	16.6%	17.3%	18.7%	19.1%	19.2%					
OMB FY20 1 1 Current Policy Baseline, 7/20 10					14.6%	16.4%	17.4%	17.9%	18.7%	18.6%	19.0%	19.3%	19.4%	19.6%	19.6%
OMB FY20 1 1 BEA Baseline, 7/2010					14.6%	17.7%	18.9%	19.5%	20.3%	20.3%	20.8%	21.1%	21.4%	21.6%	21.7%
President's FY20 11 Budget, MSR 7/2010					14.6%	17.5%	18.7%	19.4%	20.1%	20.1%	20.4%	20.6%	20.8%	20.9%	21.0%
CBO Rev. Baseline 8/2010					14.6%	17.5%	18.7%	19.4%	20.1%	20.1%	20.4%	20.6%	20.8%	20.9%	21.0%

Sources: CBO and OMB

Notes: OMB data are divided by OMB GDP estimates; CBO data by CBO GDP estimates. See source documents and text for additional caveats. "CBO Rev. Baseline 3/2010" data are taken from March 5, 2010, preliminary analysis.

On March 5, 2010, CBO published a preliminary analysis of the President's FY2011 proposals.[21] CBO issued a more detailed analysis on March 24, which incorporated legislative changes made before mid-March 2010, although the projections of budget aggregates were only slightly changed.[22] The March CBO budget projections do not reflect enactment of either the Hiring Incentives to Restore Employment Act (HIRE; P.L. 111-147) or the Patient Protection and Affordable Care Act (P.L. 111-148).

Administration proposals, according to CBO analysis, would lead to larger federal deficits over the 10-year FY20 11 -FY2020 budget window than those projected by the Obama Administration, in large part because CBO projects that the economy would grow more slowly than does OMB. CBO and OMB projections of gross domestic product (GDP) are presented in **Table 11**. A section following that table discusses some technical challenges of budget forecasting.

PROJECTIONS OF FEDERAL REVENUES

Administration and CBO projections of the future path of federal receipts are summarized in **Table 2**. Because economic conditions strongly affect federal revenue streams, forecasts of federal receipts beyond the short term are necessarily imprecise. Economic recession caused federal receipts to fall sharply in FY2008 and FY2009. Federal revenues fell 17% between FY2007 and FY2009. Receipts in FY2010 are expected to reflect renewed economic growth, and a modest rebound is expected in FY2011.

Corporate tax receipts and capital gains receipts can be especially sensitive to cyclical economic conditions. Asset values and corporate profits—and thus federal corporate income tax and capital gains revenues—typically recover more quickly after economic downturns than lagging indicators such as unemployment.

Several major legislative initiatives enacted in the past two years included tax provisions that had significant effects on federal revenues. The American Recovery and Reinvestment Act of 2009 introduced a temporary Making Work Pay tax credit, included a one-year AMT patch, and altered rules affecting business depreciation and the treatment of cancelled debts. The Children's Health Insurance Program Reauthorization Act of 2009 (P.L. 111-3) raised certain tobacco taxes to help fund the expansion of the State Children's Health Insurance Program (CHIP).[23]

Table 3. Federal Outlays Estimates and Projections for the FY2011 budget: Billions of Current Dollars and as % of GDP

Outlays	FY 2006	FY 2007	FY 2008	FY 2009	FY 2010	FY 2011	FY 2012	FY 2013	FY 2014	FY 2015	FY 2016	FY 2017	FY 2018	FY 2019	FY 2020
Historical	2,655	2,729	2,983	3,518											
CBO Baseline, 1/2010					3,524	3,650	3,613	3,756	3,940	4,105	4,335	4,521	4,712	5,000	5,250
President's FY20 11 Budget, 2/09					3,721	3,834	3,755	3,915	4,161	4,386	4,665	4,872	5,084	5,415	5,713
OMB FY2011 Current Policy Baseline, 2/2010					3,643	3,728	3,762	3,973	4,203	4,400	4,661	4,879	5,103	5,443	5,746
OMB FY2011 BEA					3,635	3,694	3,682	3,869	4,077	4,252	4,487	4,680	4,874	5,178	5,443
Baseline, 2/2010															
Prelim CBO Est. of					3,618	3,802	3,722	3,842	4,065	4,297	4,587	4,808	5,032	5,364	5,670
Pres. Budget 3/2010															
CBO Est. of Pres.					3,618	3,802	3,722	3,842	4,065	4,297	4,587	4,808	5,032	5,364	5,670
Budget 3/24/2010															
CBO Rev. Baseline 3/2010					3,537	3,668	3,608	3,746	3,931	4,100	4,330	4,520	4,707	4,996	5,250
CBO Rev. Baseline 3/24/2010					3,545	3,668	3,609	3,746	3,931	4,101	4,331	4,521	4,708	4,996	5,251
Budget Resolution-S Budget 4/2010					3,567	3,770	3,637	3,724	3,933	4,127					
President's FY2011 Budget, MSR 7/2010					3,603	3,842	3,725	3,838	4,139	4,359	4,610	4,804	5,051	5,345	5,626

Table 3. (Continued)

Outlays	FY 2006	FY 2007	FY 2008	FY 2009	FY 2010	FY 2011	FY 2012	FY 2013	FY 2014	FY 2015	FY 2016	FY 2017	FY 2018	FY 2019	FY 2020
OMB FY2011 Current Policy Baseline, 7/20 10					3,547	3,711	3,715	3,901	4,216	4,448	4,711	4,916	5,177	5,486	5,776
OMB FY2011 BEA Baseline, 7/20 10					3,546	3,694	3,649	3,805	4,094	4,303	4,542	4,721	4,952	5,226	5,479
CBO Rev. Baseline 8/2010					3,485	3,714	3,618	3,760	4,000	4,250	4,560	4,780	4,983	5,274	5,541
Historical	20.1%	19.6%	20.7%	24.7%											
CBO Baseline, 1/2010					24.1%	24.3%	23.0%	22.5%	22.4%	22.3%	22.6%	22.6%	22.6%	23.1%	23.3%
President's FY2011 Budget, 2/09					25.4%	25.1%	23.2%	22.8%	22.9%	22.9%	23.1%	23.1%	23.0%	23.5%	23.7%
OMB FY2011 Current Policy Baseline, 2/2010					24.9%	24.4%	23.2%	23.1%	23.1%	22.9%	23.1%	23.1%	23.1%	23.6%	23.9%
OMB FY2011 BEA Baseline, 2/2010					24.9%	24.1%	22.7%	22.5%	22.4%	22.2%	22.3%	22.1%	22.1%	22.4%	22.6%
Prelim CBO Est. of Pres. Budget 3/2010					24.8%	25.4%	23.7%	23.0%	23.1%	23.3%	23.9%	24.0%	24.2%	24.8%	25.2%
CBO Est. of Pres. Budget 3/24/2010					24.8%	25.4%	23.7%	23.0%	23.1%	23.3%	23.9%	24.0%	24.2%	24.8%	25.2%
CBO Rev. Baseline 3/2010					24.2%	24.5%	22.9%	22.5%	22.3%	22.3%	22.5%	22.6%	22.6%	23.1%	23.3%
CBO Rev. Baseline 3/24/2010					24.3%	24.5%	22.9%	22.5%	22.3%	22.3%	22.5%	22.6%	22.6%	23.1%	23.3%

Table 3. (Continued)

Outlays	FY 2006	FY 2007	FY 2008	FY 2009	FY 2010	FY 2011	FY 2012	FY 2013	FY 2014	FY 2015	FY 2016	FY 2017	FY 2018	FY 2019	FY 2020
Budget Resolution-S Budget 4/2010					24.3%	24.9%	23.1%	22.3%	22.1%	22.2%	—	—	—	—	—
President's FY2011 Budget, MSR 7/2010					24.6%	25.4%	23.6%	23.0%	23.3%	23.4%	23.6%	23.5%	23.7%	24.1%	24.3%
OMB FY2011 Current Policy Baseline, 7/2010					24.2%	24.5%	23.6%	23.4%	23.7%	23.9%	24.1%	24.1%	24.3%	24.7%	24.9%
OMB FY2011 BEA Baseline, 7/2010					24.2%	24.4%	23.1%	22.8%	23.1%	23.1%	23.3%	23.1%	23.3%	23.5%	23.7%
CBO Rev. Baseline 8/2010					23.8%	24.5%	23.0%	22.5%	22.5%	22.8%	23.4%	23.4%	23.4%	23.8%	23.9%

Sources: CBO and OMB

Notes: OMB data are divided by OMB GDP estimates; CBO data by CBO GDP estimates. See source documents and text for additional caveats. "CBO Rev. Baseline 3/2010" data are taken from March 5, 2010, preliminary analysis.

Updated CBO and OMB estimates predict that federal revenues as a share of GDP in FY2010 (14.6%) will be slightly less than in FY2009 (14.8%). The CBO baseline forecast for FY2011 expects economic recovery to boost federal revenues to 17.5% of GDP. At the end of the 10-year budget window, federal revenues are projected to be just over one-fifth of GDP (21.0% in FY2020). All projections shown in **Table 2** project that FY20 11 revenues will exceed FY20 10 revenues.

FEDERAL OUTLAYS

Outlays and Budget Authority

Many budget documents also report spending in terms of budget authority, which specifies what federal agencies can legally spend. Budget authority has been compared to funds deposited into a checking account, which then can be used for specified federal purposes. Congress often sets time limits on the availability of budget authority, although some accounts contain "no-year" funds that do not automatically expire. Federal agencies with available budget authority can obligate funds by signing contracts, hiring employees, or by entering into other binding agreements. Until the federal government disburses funds to make purchases, however, no outlays occur. Outlays will not increase until those funds are actually disbursed. Budget authority that is not obligated, aside from "no-year" funds, expires once the period of availability ends.[24]

Outlay data are more convenient for assessing the macroeconomic effects of the federal budgets, while analysts focusing on specific federal programs typically rely on budget authority figures. Appropriations legislation is generally framed in terms of budget authority, because Congress can control the amount of funds made available for specific purposes. The timing of federal outlays, on the other hand, often depends on administrative decisions of federal program officials, made within bounds set by Congress. This chapter focuses on outlays, rather than budget authority, in order to highlight broader effects of the federal budget on the economy.

Federal Outlay Projections

Table 3 summarizes Administration and CBO projections of future federal outlays (i.e., disbursed federal funds). Federal spending is projected to account for about a quarter of the U.S. economy in FY20 11. In FY2008, federal spending accounted for just over one-fifth (20.9%) of the U.S. economy, nearly equal to its average share of gross domestic product (GDP) since FY1962.

The Administration's budget submission calls for FY20 11 outlays of $3,834 billion (25.1% of GDP), $166 billion above the March 2010 CBO baseline. Those baseline projections show outlays rising from $3,537 billion in FY20 10 to $3,668 billion in FY20 11. CBO estimates that outlays under the President's budget plans would total $3,802 billion in FY20 11 and $3,722 billion in FY20 12.

The Obama Administration outlay projections include an estimate of future disaster costs, which is not included in either discretionary or mandatory spending projections. These estimates, shown in **Table 4**, serve as budgetary "plugs" rather than projections of disaster costs in particular years. Thus, for both the OMB projections reflecting the President's budget proposals and the OMB current policy baseline, estimated future disaster costs would need to be added to discretionary outlays, mandatory outlays, and net interest in order to equal total outlays.

Discretionary Outlays

Discretionary spending is provided and controlled through appropriations acts, which fund many of the activities commonly associated with such federal government functions as running executive branch agencies, congressional offices and agencies, and international operations of the government.[25] Essentially all spending on federal wages and salaries is discretionary.

Table 4. Administration Estimates of Expected Costs of Future Federal Costs of Disaster Assistance Billions of Current Dollars by Fiscal Year

2010	2011	2012	2013	2014	2015	2016	2017	2018	2019	2020
0.625	2.250	3.625	4.125	4.375	4.625	4.875	5.000	5.000	5.000	5.000

Source: OMB Notes: See text.

Table 5 presents projections of discretionary outlays. While discretionary spending was the largest category of federal spending until the mid-1970s, mandatory spending in FY2010 (13.1% of GDP) accounted for about 4% more of GDP than discretionary spending (9.3% of GDP) according to August 2010 CBO estimates.[26] Discretionary spending will decline to just 7.0% of GDP in FY2020, according to CBO baseline projections, which assume that discretionary spending is held constant in inflation-adjusted terms.

Discretionary spending over the next several fiscal years is projected to decrease in inflation- adjusted terms. The Obama Administration has called for a three-year freeze on non-security discretionary spending. The Obama Administration essentially defines "security" spending as funding for the Department of Defense, the Department of Energy's National Nuclear Security Administration, the Department of Homeland Security, the Department of Veterans Affairs, the Department of State, and international food aid programs.[27] The Obama Administration has proposed moving funding for some Pell Grants, which are aimed at post-secondary education students that meet certain eligibility and financial need requirements, from discretionary spending to mandatory spending.[28]

Mandatory Outlays

Mandatory spending includes federal government spending on entitlement programs and the Supplemental Nutrition Assistance Program (SNAP; formerly Food Stamps) as well as other budget outlays controlled by laws other than appropriation acts.[29] Entitlement programs such as Social Security and Medicare make up the bulk of mandatory spending. Other mandatory spending programs include Temporary Assistance for Needy Families (TANF), Supplemental Security Income (S SI), unemployment insurance, some veterans' benefits, federal employee retirement and disability, and the earned income tax credit (EITC).

Table 6 summarizes projections of mandatory outlays. According to August 2010 CBO baseline estimates, mandatory outlays will total $2,085 billion (13.8% of GDP) in FY2011 and $1,971 billion (12.5% of GDP) in FY2012.

Table 5. Federal Discretionary Outlays Estimates and Projections for the FY2011 Budget: Billions of Current Dollars and as % of GDP

Discretionary Outlays	FY 2007	FY 2008	FY 2009	FY 2010	FY 2011	FY 2012	FY 2013	FY 2014	FY 2015	FY 2016	FY 2017	FY 2018	FY 2019	FY 2020
Historical	1,041	1,135	1,219											
CBO Baseline, 1/2010			1,237	1,371	1,371	1,344	1,346	1,357	1,373	1,402	1,426	1,450	1,486	1,518
President's FY2011 Budget, 2/09			1,219	1,408	1,415	1,301	1,267	1,283	1,310	1,337	1,371	1,405	1,442	1,484
OMB FY2011 Current Policy Baseline, 2/2010			1,219	1,397	1,376	1,340	1,343	1,367	1,396	1,425	1,460	1,496	1,534	1,573
OMB FY2011 BEA Baseline, 2/2010			1,238	1,424	1,396	1,360	1,364	1,388	1,418	1,447	1,482	1,519	1,557	1,597
Prelim CBO Est. of Pres. Budget 3/20 10			1,237	1,375	1,401	1,334	1,301	1,303	1,323	1,355	1,381	1,407	1,446	1,487
CBO Est. of Pres. Budget 3/24/20 10			1,237	1,375	1,401	1,334	1,301	1,303	1,323	1,355	1,381	1,407	1,446	1,487
CBO Rev. Baseline 3/2010			1,237	1,367	1,373	1,344	1,345	1,356	1,372	1,401	1,425	1,449	1,484	1,517
CBO Rev. Baseline 3/24/2010				1,367	1,373	1,345	1,345	1,356	1,372	1,401	1,425	1,449	1,484	1,517
Budget Resolution – S Budget 4/2010				1,377	1,413	1,347	1,311	1,304	1,316					
President's FY2011 Budget, MSR 7/2010			1,219	1,377	1,433	1,316	1,274	1,284	1,309	1,339	1,375	1,406	1,443	1,486
OMB FY2011 Current Policy Baseline, 7/2010			1,219	1,364	1,394	1,354	1,352	1,371	1,399	1,429	1,466	1,499	1,537	1,576
OMB FY2011 BEA Baseline, 7/2010			1,219	1,393	1,419	1,375	1,373	1,392	1,421	1,452	1,489	1,523	1,561	1,600

Table 5. (Continued)

Discretionary Outlays	FY 2007	FY 2008	FY 2009	FY 2010	FY 2011	FY 2012	FY 2013	FY 2014	FY 2015	FY 2016	FY 2017	FY 2018	FY 2019	FY 2020
CBO Rev. Baseline 8/2010				1,358	1,404	1,388	1,399	1,418	1,443	1,481	1,511	1,542	1,584	1,622
As % GDP														
OMB/Historical/Actual FY2009	7.6%	7.9%	8.6%											
CBO Baseline, 1/2010			8.7%	9.4%	9.1%	8.5%	8.1%	7.7%	7.5%	7.3%	7.1%	7.0%	6.9%	6.7%
President's FY2011 Budget, 2/09			8.6%	9.6%	9.2%	8.0%	7.4%	7.1%	6.8%	6.6%	6.5%	6.4%	6.3%	6.2%
OMB FY2011 Current Policy Baseline, 2/2010			8.6%	9.6%	9.0%	8.3%	7.8%	7.5%	7.3%	7.1%	6.9%	6.8%	6.6%	6.5%
OMB FY2011 BEA Baseline, 2/2010			8.7%	9.7%	9.1%	8.4%	7.9%	7.6%	7.4%	7.2%	7.0%	6.9%	6.8%	6.6%
Prelim CBO Est. of Pres. Budget 3/2010			8.7%	9.4%	9.3%	8.5%	7.8%	7.4%	7.2%	7.0%	6.9%	6.8%	6.7%	6.6%
CBO Est. of Pres. Budget 3/24/2010				9.4%	9.3%	8.5%	7.8%	7.4%	7.2%	7.0%	6.9%	6.8%	6.7%	6.6%
CBO Rev. Baseline 3/2010				9.4%	9.2%	8.5%	8.1%	7.7%	7.4%	7.3%	7.1%	7.0%	6.9%	6.7%
CBO Rev. Baseline 3/24/2010				9.4%	9.2%	8.5%	8.1%	7.7%	7.4%	7.3%	7.1%	7.0%	6.9%	6.7%
President's FY2011 Budget, MSR 7/2010				9.4%	9.5%	8.3%	7.6%	7.2%	7.0%	6.9%	6.7%	6.6%	6.5%	6.4%
Budget Resolution - S Budget 4/2010				9.4%	9.3%	8.5%	7.8%	7.3%	7.1%	—	—	—	—	—
OMB FY2011 Current Policy Baseline, 7/2010				9.3%	9.2%	8.6%	8.1%	7.7%	7.5%	7.3%	7.2%	7.0%	6.9%	6.8%
OMB FY2011 BEA Baseline, 7/2010				9.5%	9.4%	8.7%	8.2%	7.8%	7.6%	7.4%	7.3%	7.2%	7.0%	6.9%

Table 5. (Continued)

Discretionary Outlays	FY 2007	FY 2008	FY 2009	FY 2010	FY 2011	FY 2012	FY 2013	FY 2014	FY 2015	FY 2016	FY 2017	FY 2018	FY 2019	FY 2020
CBO Rev. Baseline 8/2010				9.3%	9.3%	8.8%	8.4%	8.0%	7.7%	7.6%	7.4%	7.2%	7.1%	7.0%

Sources: CBO and OMB

Notes: OMB does not break out some future disaster spending estimates between mandatory and discretionary spending. OMB data are divided by OMB GDP estimates; CBO data by CBO GDP estimates. "CBO Rev. Baseline 3/2010" data are from March 5, 2010, preliminary analysis. See source documents and text for additional caveats.

Table 6. Federal Mandatory Outlays Estimates and projections for the FY20 1 1 budget: Billions of Current Dollars and as % of GDP

Mandatory Outlays	FY 2006	FY 2007	FY 2008	FY 2009	FY 2010	FY 2011	FY 2012	FY 2013	FY 2014	FY 2015	FY 2016	FY 2017	FY 2018	FY 2019	FY 2020
OMB/Historical/ Actual FY2009	1,412	1,451	1,848	2,112											
CBO Baseline, 1/2010				2,094	1,946	2,045	1,989	2,077	2,188	2,272	2,414	2,524	2,638	2,838	3,008
President's FY2011 Budget, 2/09				2,112	2,123	2,165	2,107	2,208	2,364	2,500	2,696	2,815	2,942	3,182	3,384
OMB FY2011 Current Policy Baseline, 2/2010				2,112	2,057	2,100	2,079	2,191	2,316	2,413	2,579	2,698	2,823	3,060	3,256
OMB FY2011 BEA Baseline, 2/2010				2,093	2,023	2,050	1,993	2,101	2,224	2,319	2,483	2,600	2,721	2,951	3,142
Prelim CBO Est. of Pres. Budget 3/2010				2,094	2,034	2,157	2,091	2,176	2,322	2,454	2,636	2,752	2,871	3,084	3,267

Table 6. (Continued)

Mandatory Outlays	FY 2006	FY 2007	FY 2008	FY 2009	FY 2010	FY 2011	FY 2012	FY 2013	FY 2014	FY 2015	FY 2016	FY 2017	FY 2018	FY 2019	FY 2020
CBO Est. of Pres. Budget 3/24/2010				2,094	2,034	2,156	2,091	2,176	2,322	2,454	2,636	2,752	2,871	3,084	3,267
CBO Rev. Baseline 3/2010				2,094	1,961	2,058	1,982	2,063	2,177	2,267	2,412	2,523	2,633	2,834	3,005
CBO Rev. Baseline 3/24/20 10					1,969	2,058	1,982	2,063	2,177	2,267	2,412	2,523	2,633	2,834	3,005
Budget Resolution – S Budget 4/2010					1,981	2,116	1,998	2,058	2,207	2,320					
President's FY2011 Budget, MSR 7/2010				2,112	2,041	2,186	2,112	2,175	2,371	2,491	2,649	2,749	2,911	3,117	3,304
OMB FY2011 Current Policy Baseline, 7/20 10				2,112	1,997	2,094	2,066	2,163	2,359	2,480	2,639	2,738	2,901	3,107	3,295
OMB FY2011 BEA Baseline, 7/2010				2,112	1,969	2,055	1,988	2,071	2,265	2,384	2,540	2,637	2,796	2,996	3,178
CBO Rev. Baseline 8/2010				2,093	1,925	2,085	1,971	2,035	2,172	2,316	2,515	2,646	2,766	2,964	3,141
As % GDP															
OMB/Historical/ Actual FY2009	10.7%	10.4%	12.8%	14.8%											
CBO Baseline, 1/2010				14.7%	13.3%	13.6%	12.6%	12.5%	12.4%	12.3%	12.6%	12.6%	12.7%	13.1%	13.3%
President's FY2011 Budget, 2/09				14.8%	14.5%	14.2%	13.0%	12.9%	13.0%	13.0%	13.4%	13.3%	13.3%	13.8%	14.1%
OMB FY2011 Current Policy Baseline, 2/2010				14.8%	14.1%	13.7%	12.8%	12.8%	12.7%	12.6%	12.8%	12.8%	12.8%	13.3%	13.5%
OMB FY2011 BEA Baseline, 2/2010				14.7%	13.8%	13.4%	12.3%	12.2%	12.2%	12.1%	12.3%	12.3%	12.3%	12.8%	13.1%

Table 6. (Continued)

Mandatory Outlays	FY 2006	FY 2007	FY 2008	FY 2009	FY 2010	FY 2011	FY 2012	FY 2013	FY 2014	FY 2015	FY 2016	FY 2017	FY 2018	FY 2019	FY 2020
Prelim CBO Est. of Pres. Budget 3/2010				14.7%	13.9%	14.4%	13.3%	13.0%	13.2%	13.3%	13.7%	13.7%	13.8%	14.2%	14.5%
CBO Est. of Pres. Budget 3/24/2010					13.9%	14.4%	13.3%	13.0%	13.2%	13.3%	13.7%	13.7%	13.8%	14.2%	14.5%
CBO Rev. Baseline 3/2010					13.4%	13.7%	12.6%	12.4%	12.4%	12.3%	12.5%	12.6%	12.6%	13.1%	13.3%
CBO Rev. Baseline 3/24/2010					13.5%	13.7%	12.6%	12.4%	12.4%	12.3%	12.5%	12.6%	12.6%	13.1%	13.3%
Budget Resolution - S Budget 4/2010					13.5%	14.0%	12.7%	12.3%	12.4%	12.5%	—	—	—	—	—
President's FY2011 Budget, MSR 7/2010				14.8%	13.9%	14.4%	13.4%	13.0%	13.3%	13.4%	13.6%	13.5%	13.7%	14.0%	14.3%
OMB FY2011 Current Policy Baseline, 7/2010				14.8%	13.6%	13.8%	13.1%	12.9%	13.3%	13.3%	13.5%	13.4%	13.6%	14.0%	14.2%
OMB FY2011 BEA Baseline, 7/2010				14.8%	13.4%	13.6%	12.6%	12.4%	12.8%	12.8%	13.0%	12.9%	13.1%	13.5%	13.7%
CBO Rev. Baseline 8/2010					13.1%	13.8%	12.5%	12.2%	12.2%	12.4%	12.9%	13.0%	13.0%	13.3%	13.6%

Sources: CBO and OMB

Notes: OMB does not break out some future disaster spending estimates between mandatory and discretionary spending. OMB data are divided by OMB GDP estimates; CBO data by CBO GDP estimates. "CBO Rev. Baseline 3/2010" data are from March 5, 2010, preliminary analysis. See source documents and text for additional caveats.

Most of the costs of federal interventions that responded to financial turmoil in 2007 and 2008 were classified as mandatory, which pushed mandatory spending to $2,112 billion (14.8% of GDP) in FY2009. Stabilization of financial markets is expected to lead to lower mandatory spending totals in the next few years. Rising entitlement program costs, however, are projected to lead to significant increases in mandatory spending in later years.

DEFICITS

Deficits occur when Congress and the President enact policies that cause federal spending to exceed federal receipts. Deficits increase government debt held by the public, generally increasing net interest payments. Surpluses occur when federal receipts exceed outlays, which reduces federal debt held by the public.[30] This can, in turn, reduce net interest payments.

Governments run deficits for several reasons. By running short-run deficits, governments can avoid raising taxes during economic downturns, helping households to smooth consumption over time. Running deficits can stimulate aggregate demand in the economy, giving policy makers a valuable fiscal policy tool that can help support macroeconomic stability. Long-run deficits allow transfers of economic resources from younger to older generations, enabling older generations to enjoy anticipated benefits of future economic growth, but also may be used to impose large burdens on future generations.[31]

Deficits can seriously harm national economies. Governments can spend more than they collect in revenues by printing money, which can cause inflation, or by borrowing. In the short run, fiscal overstimulation leads to inflation. In the long term, deficits either reduce capital investment, which retards economic growth, or increase foreign borrowing, which swells the share of national income going abroad. In the long run, governments that fail to repay borrowers, at least to the extent of stabilizing the ratio of government debt to gross domestic product, risk default and bankruptcy.

Table 7 summarizes Administration and CBO projections of total federal deficits. Long-term CBO and OMB projections both show substantial increases in budget deficits in the years after FY2020.[32] These deficits result from a projected gap between rising federal outlays and revenues. The growth of health care spending, as well as demographic changes, plays an important part of those fiscal trends. The federal government last ran a surplus in FY200 1, which amounted to $128 billion or 1.3% of GDP.

On-Budget Deficits and Off-Budget Surpluses

The total federal deficit (or surplus) is the sum of the off-budget and on-budget deficits or surpluses. The U.S. Postal Service net profits or losses and Social Security revenues net of beneficiary payments are by law considered off-budget entities.

Table 8 summarizes projections of on-budget deficits. The on-budget deficit is estimated to decline to $1,154 billion (7.6% of GDP) in FY20 11 according to CBO August 2010 baseline projections. None of the projections show an on-budget surplus within the next 5 or 10 years.

Table 9 summarizes projections of off-budget surpluses, which mainly comprise Social Security surpluses. Since FY1985, Social Security surpluses have led to off-budget surpluses, which has reduced the size of the total deficit. High unemployment rates and other effects of economic recession have lowered inflows of payroll taxes, pushing off-budget surpluses below previously expected levels.

FEDERAL DEBT

Gross federal debt is the sum of debt held by the public and intragovernmental (IG) debt.[33] IG debt is the amount owed by the federal government to other federal agencies, which the U.S. Treasury is obligated to pay at some future time. The Social Security and Medicare trust funds, which by law must be invested in federal securities, are the largest components of IG debt.[34] IG debt also includes dozens of other federal trust funds.[35]

Debt held by the public is the total amount the federal government has borrowed from the public and remains outstanding. This measure is generally considered to be the most relevant in macroeconomic terms because it is the amount of debt sold in credit markets. Table 10 shows various projections of debt held by the public.

Table 7. Total Deficits Estimates and projections for the FY2011 budget: Billions of Current Dollars and as % of GDP

Total Deficits	FY 2006	FY 2007	FY 2008	FY 2009	FY 2010	FY 2011	FY 2012	FY 2013	FY 2014	FY 2015	FY 2016	FY 2017	FY 2018	FY 2019	FY 2020
OMB/Historical/ Actual FY2009	-248	-161	-459	-1,413											
CBO Baseline, 1/2010					-1,349	-980	-650	-539	-475	-480	-521	-525	-542	-649	-687
President's FY2011 Budget, 2/09					-1,556	-1,267	-828	-727	-706	-752	-778	-778	-785	-908	-1,003
OMB FY2011 Current Policy Baseline, 2/2010					-1,430	-1,145	-934	-940	-934	-983	-1,013	-1,042	-1,077	-1,227	-1,346
OMB FY2011 BEA Baseline, 2/2010					-1,404	-912	-613	-561	-495	-492	-469	-445	-421	-507	-557
Prelim CBO Est. of Pres. Budget 3/2010					-1,500	-1,341	-915	-747	-724	-793	-894	-940	-1,001	-1,152	-1,253
CBO Est. of Pres. Budget 3/24/2010					-1,500	-1,342	-914	-747	-724	-793	-894	-940	-996	-1,152	-1,254
CBO Rev. Baseline 3/2010					-1,360	-995	-641	-525	-462	-471	-512	-520	-533	-640	-683
CBO Rev. Baseline 3/24/2010					-1,368	-996	-642	-525	-463	-472	-513	-521	-534	-641	-684
Budget Resolution – S Budget 4/2010					-1,415	-1,260	-902	-593	-548	-544					

Table 7. (Continued)

Total Deficits	FY 2006	FY 2007	FY 2008	FY 2009	FY 2010	FY 2011	FY 2012	FY 2013	FY 2014	FY 2015	FY 2016	FY 2017	FY 2018	FY 2019	FY 2020
President's FY2011 Budget, MSR 7/2010					-1,471	-1,416	-911	-736	-698	-762	-758	-721	-749	-822	-900
OMB FY2011 Current Policy Baseline, 7/20 10					-1,405	-1,233	-967	-904	-896	-985	-1,003	-987	-1,037	-1,132	-1,230
OMB FY2011 BEA Baseline, 7/2010					-1,404	-1,012	-668	-546	-481	-514	-478	-408	-401	-433	-464
CBO Rev. Baseline 8/2010					-1,342	-1,066	-665	-525	-438	-507	-585	-579	-562	-634	-685
As % GDP															
OMB/Historical/ Actual FY2009	-1.9%	-1.2%	-3.2%	-9.9%											
CBO Baseline, 1/2010					-9.2%	-6.5%	-4.1%	-3.2%	-2.7%	-2.6%	-2.7%	-2.6%	-2.6%	-3.0%	-3.0%
President's FY2011 Budget, 2/09					-10.6%	-8.3%	-5.1%	-4.2%	-3.9%	-3.9%	-3.9%	-3.7%	-3.6%	-3.9%	-4.2%
OMB FY2011 Current Policy Baseline, 2/2010					-10.6%	-8.3%	-5.1%	-4.2%	-3.9%	-3.9%	-3.9%	-3.7%	-3.6%	-3.9%	-4.2%
OMB FY2011 BEA Baseline, 2/2010					-10.6%	-8.3%	-5.1%	-4.2%	-3.9%	-3.9%	-3.9%	-3.7%	-3.6%	-3.9%	-4.2%
Prelim CBO Est. of Pres. Budget 3/2010					-10.3%	-8.9%	-5.8%	-4.5%	-4.1%	-4.3%	-4.7%	-4.7%	-4.8%	-5.3%	-5.6%
CBO Est. of Pres. Budget 3/24/2010					-10.3%	-8.9%	-5.8%	-4.5%	-4.1%	-4.3%	-4.7%	-4.7%	-4.8%	-5.3%	-5.6%

Table 7. (Continued)

Total Deficits	FY 2006	FY 2007	FY 2008	FY 2009	FY 2010	FY 2011	FY 2012	FY 2013	FY 2014	FY 2015	FY 2016	FY 2017	FY 2018	FY 2019	FY 2020
CBO Rev. Baseline 3/2010					-9.3%	-6.6%	-4.1%	-3.1%	-2.6%	-2.6%	-2.7%	-2.6%	-2.6%	-3.0%	-3.0%
CBO Rev. Baseline 3/24/2010					-9.4%	-6.6%	-4.1%	-3.1%	-2.6%	-2.6%	-2.7%	-2.6%	-2.6%	-3.0%	-3.0%
Budget Resolution – S Budget 4/2010					-9.6%	-8.3%	-5.7%	-3.6%	-3.1%	-2.9%	—	—	—	—	—
President's FY2011 Budget, MSR 7/2010					-10.0%	-9.3%	-5.8%	-4.4%	-3.9%	-4.1%	-3.9%	-3.5%	-3.5%	-3.7%	-3.9%
OMB FY2011 Current Policy Baseline, 7/2010					-9.6%	-8.1%	-6.1%	-5.4%	-5.0%	-5.3%	-5.1%	-4.8%	-4.9%	-5.1%	-5.3%
OMB FY2011 BEA Baseline, 7/2010					-9.6%	-6.7%	-4.2%	-3.3%	-2.7%	-2.8%	-2.4%	-2.0%	-1.9%	-2.0%	-2.0%
CBO Rev. Baseline 8/2010					-9.1%	-7.0%	-4.2%	-3.1%	-2.5%	-2.7%	-3.0%	-2.8%	-2.6%	-2.9%	-3.0%

Sources: CBO and OMB

Notes: OMB data are divided by OMB GDP estimates; CBO data by CBO GDP estimates. "CBO Rev. Baseline 3/20 10" data are taken from March 5, 2010, preliminary analysis. See source documents and text for additional caveats.

Table 8. On-Budget Deficits Estimates and Projections for the FY2011 Budget: Billions of Current Dollars and as % of GDP

On-Budget Deficits	FY2006	FY2007	FY2008	FY2009	FY2010	FY201 1	FY2012	FY2013	FY2014	FY2015	FY2016
OMB/Historical/Actual FY2009	-435	-342	-638	-1,550							
CBO Baseline, 1/20 10					-1,434	-1,076	-757	-659	-608	-619	-659
President's FY20 11 Budget, 2/09					-1,634	-1,363	-949	-863	-852	-910	-952
OMB FY201 1 Current Policy Baseline, 2/2010					-1,508	-1,241	-1,054	-1,074	-1,080	-1,139	-1,183
OMB FY20 1 1 BEA Baseline, 2/2010					-1,482	-1,008	-733	-695	-642	-648	-640
Prelim CBO Est. of Pres. Budget 3/2010					-1,585	-1,435	-1,020	-865	-854	-931	-1,033
CBO Est. of Pres. Budget 3/24/2010					-1,585	-1,435	-1,019	-865	-853	-931	-1,033
CBO Rev. Baseline 3/2010					-1,444	-1,089	-747	-642	-593	-609	-648
CBO Rev. Baseline 3/24/2010					-1,453	-1,089	-747	-643	-593	-609	-649
Budget Resolution - S Budget 4/2010					-1,499	-1,353	-1,007	-711	-679	-682	—
President's FY20 11 Budget, MSR 7/2010					-1,545	-1,495	-1,015	-851	-823	-895	-904
OMB FY201 1 Current Policy Baseline, 7/2010					-1,479	-1,312	-1,071	-1,019	-1,021	-1,118	-1,148
OMB FY20 1 1 BEA Baseline, 7/20 10					-1,478	-1,091	-773	-661	-607	-647	-623

Table 8. (Continued)

On-Budget Deficits	FY2006	FY2007	FY2008	FY2009	FY2010	FY201 1	FY2012	FY2013	FY2014	FY2015	FY2016
CBO Rev. Baseline 8/20 10					-1,419	-1,154	-766	-639	-569	-650	-732
As % GDP											
OMB/Historical/Actual FY2009	-3.3%	-2.5%	-4.4%	- 10.9%							
CBO Baseline, 1/2010					-9.8%	-7.2%	-4.8%	-4.0%	-3.5%	-3.4%	-3.4%
President's FY20 11 Budget, 2/09					- 11.2%	-8.9%	-5.9%	-5.0%	-4.7%	-4.7%	-4.7%
OMB FY20 1 1 Current Policy Baseline, 2/20 10					-10.3%	-8.1%	-6.5%	-6.3%	-5.9%	-5.9%	-5.9%
OMB FY20 1 1 BEA Baseline, 2/20 10					-10.1%	-6.6%	-4.5%	-4.0%	-3.5%	-3.4%	-3.2%
Prelim CBO Est. of Pres. Budget 3/2010					- 10.9%	-9.6%	-6.5%	-5.2%	-4.8%	-5.1%	-5.4%
CBO Est. of Pres. Budget 3/24/2010					- 10.9%	-9.6%	-6.5%	-5.2%	-4.8%	-5.1%	-5.4%
CBO Rev. Baseline 3/2010					-9.9%	-7.3%	-4.7%	-3.9%	-3.4%	-3.3%	-3.4%
CBO Rev. Baseline 3/24/2010					- 10.0%	-7.3%	-4.8%	-3.9%	-3.4%	-3.3%	-3.4%
President's FY2011 Budget, MSR 7/2010					-10.5%	-9.9%	-6.4%	-5.1%	-4.6%	-4.8%	-4.6%
Budget Resolution - S Budget 4/2010					-10.2%	-8.9%	-6.4%	-4.3%	-3.8%	-3.7%	—
OMB FY2011 Current Policy Baseline, 7/2010					-10.1%	-8.7%	-6.8%	-6.1%	-5.8%	-6.0%	-5.9%

Table 8. (Continued)

On-Budget Deficits	FY2006	FY2007	FY2008	FY2009	FY2010	FY201 1	FY2012	FY2013	FY2014	FY2015	FY2016
OMB FY2011 BEA Baseline, 7/2010					-10.1%	-7.2%	-4.9%	-4.0%	-3.4%	-3.5%	-3.2%
CBO Rev. Baseline 8/2010					-9.7%	-7.6%	-4.9%	-3.8%	-3.2%	-3.5%	-3.8%

Sources: CBO and OMB

Notes: OMB data are divided by OMB GDP estimates; CBO data by CBO GDP estimates. "CBO Rev. Baseline 3/20 10" data are taken from March 5, 2010, preliminary analysis. See source documents and text for additional caveats.

Table 9. Off-Budget Surplus Estimates and Projections for the FY2011 Budget: Billions of Current Dollars and as % of GDP

	FY 2006	FY 2007	FY 2008	FY 2009	FY 2010	FY 2011	FY 2012	FY 2013	FY 2014	FY 2015	FY 2016	FY 2017	FY 2018	FY 2019	FY 2020
OMB/Historical/Actual FY2009	186	181	183	137											
CBO Baseline, 1/2010					86	96	108	120	133	139	138	134	127	116	107
President's FY2011 Budget, 2/09					78	96	120	136	146	158	175	174	174	167	151
OMB FY2011 Current Policy Baseline, 2/2010					78	96	120	135	147	156	170	168	166	157	140
OMB FY2011 BEA Baseline, 2/2010					78	96	121	135	147	156	170	168	166	158	140
Prelim CBO Est. of Pres. Budget 3/2010					85	93	105	118	130	138	139	136	130	121	112
CBO Est. of Pres. Budget 3/24/2010					85	93	105	118	130	138	139	136	130	121	112
CBO Rev. Baseline 3/2010					85	94	106	118	131	137	136	131	124	113	102
CBO Rev. Baseline 3/24/20 10					85	94	106	118	131	137	136	131	124	113	102
Budget Resolution – S Budget 4/2010					85	93	105	118	131	138	—	—	—	—	—

Table 9. (Continued)

	FY 2006	FY 2007	FY 2008	FY 2009	FY 2010	FY 2011	FY 2012	FY 2013	FY 2014	FY 2015	FY 2016	FY 2017	FY 2018	FY 2019	FY 2020
President's FY2011 Budget, MSR 7/2010					74	79	104	115	126	133	146	144	141	133	117
OMB FY2011 Current Policy Baseline, 7/2010					74	79	104	115	125	132	145	141	138	130	113
OMB FY2011 BEA Baseline, 7/2010					74	79	104	115	126	133	145	142	138	131	114
CBO Rev. Baseline 8/2010					77	88	101	114	131	143	148	148	149	143	132
As % GDP															
OMB/Historical/Actual FY2009	1.4%	1.3%	1.3%	1.0%											
CBO Baseline, 1/2010					0.6%	0.6%	0.7%	0.7%	0.8%	0.8%	0.7%	0.7%	0.6%	0.5%	0.5%
President's FY2011 Budget, 2/09					0.5%	0.6%	0.7%	0.8%	0.8%	0.8%	0.9%	0.8%	0.8%	0.7%	0.6%
OMB FY2011 Current Policy Baseline, 2/2010					0.5%	0.6%	0.7%	0.8%	0.8%	0.8%	0.8%	0.8%	0.8%	0.7%	0.6%
OMB FY2011 BEA Baseline, 2/2010					0.5%	0.6%	0.7%	0.8%	0.8%	0.8%	0.8%	0.8%	0.8%	0.7%	0.6%
Prelim CBO Est. of Pres. Budget 3/2010					0.6%	0.6%	0.7%	0.7%	0.7%	0.8%	0.7%	0.7%	0.6%	0.6%	0.5%
CBO Est. of Pres. Budget 3/24/2010					0.6%	0.6%	0.7%	0.7%	0.7%	0.8%	0.7%	0.7%	0.6%	0.6%	0.5%
CBO Rev. Baseline 3/2010					0.6%	0.6%	0.7%	0.7%	0.7%	0.7%	0.7%	0.7%	0.6%	0.5%	0.5%
CBO Rev. Baseline 3/24/2010					0.6%	0.6%	0.7%	0.7%	0.7%	0.7%	0.7%	0.7%	0.6%	0.5%	0.5%
Budget Resolution – S Budget 4/2010					0.6%	0.6%	0.7%	0.7%	0.7%	0.7%	—	—	—	—	—
President's FY2011 Budget, MSR 7/2010					0.5%	0.5%	0.7%	0.7%	0.7%	0.7%	0.7%	0.7%	0.7%	0.6%	0.5%
OMB FY2011 Current Policy Baseline, 7/2010					0.5%	0.5%	0.7%	0.7%	0.7%	0.7%	0.7%	0.7%	0.6%	0.6%	0.5%

Table 9. (Continued)

	FY 2006	FY 2007	FY 2008	FY 2009	FY 2010	FY 2011	FY 2012	FY 2013	FY 2014	FY 2015	FY 2016	FY 2017	FY 2018	FY 2019	FY 2020
OMB FY2011 BEA Baseline, 7/2010					0.5%	0.5%	0.7%	0.7%	0.7%	0.7%	0.7%	0.7%	0.6%	0.6%	0.5%
CBO Rev. Baseline8/2010					0.5%	0.6%	0.6%	0.7%	0.7%	0.8%	0.8%	0.7%	0.7%	0.6%	0.6%

Sources: CBO and OMB

Notes: OMB data are divided by OMB GDP estimates; CBO data by CBO GDP estimates. "CBO Rev. Baseline 3/20 10" data are taken from March 5, 2010, preliminary analysis. See source documents and text for additional caveats.

Table 10. Debt Held by the Public at End of Fiscal Year Estimates and Projections for the FY2011 Budget: Billions of Current Dollars and as % of GDP

Debt Held By The Public	FY 2006	FY 2007	FY 2008	FY 2009	FY 2010	FY 2011	FY 2012	FY 2013	FY 2014	FY 2015	FY 2016	FY 2017	FY 2018	FY 2019	FY 2020
OMB/Historical/ Actual FY2009	4,829	5,035	5,803	7,545											
CBO Baseline, 1/2010					8,797	9,785	10,479	11,056	11,556	12,055	12,595	13,133	13,678	14,329	15,027
President's FY2011 Budget, 2/09					9,298	10,498	11,472	12,326	13,139	13,988	14,833	15,686	16,535	17,502	18,573
Prelim CBO Est. of Pres. Budget 3/2010					9,221	10,510	11,578	12,467	13,329	14,256	15,297	16,396	17,558	18,875	20,298
CBO Est. of Pres. Budget 3/24/2010					9,221	10,512	11,579	12,467	13,329	14,256	15,297	16,396	17,553	18,870	20,294
CBO Rev. Baseline 3/2010					9,012	9,853	10,541	11,102	11,595	12,092	12,641	13,209	13,790	14,479	15,211
CBO Rev. Baseline 3/24/20 10					9,021	9,862	10,551	11,112	11,606	12,103	12,653	13,222	13,803	14,493	15,226
Budget Resolution – S Budget 4/2010					9,067	10,173	11,122	11,752	12,331	12,900					

Table 10. (Continued)

Debt Held By The Public	FY 2006	FY 2007	FY 2008	FY 2009	FY 2010	FY 2011	FY 2012	FY 2013	FY 2014	FY 2015	FY 2016	FY 2017	FY 2018	FY 2019	FY 2020
President's FY20 11 Budget, MSR 7/2010					9,199	10,550	11,602	12,459	13,264	14,134	14,984	15,795	16,619	17,514	18,505
CBO Rev. Baseline 8/2010					9,031	10,007	10,790	11,422	11,950	12,544	13,214	13,885	14,546	15,281	16,073
As % GDP															
OMB/Historical/ Actual FY2009	36.5%	36.2%	40.2%	53.0%											
CBO Baseline, 1/2010					60.3%	65.3%	66.6%	66.3%	65.6%	65.4%	65.5%	65.5%	65.7%	66.1%	66.7%
President's FY2011 Budget, 2/09					63.6%	68.6%	70.8%	71.7%	72.2%	72.9%	73.6%	74.2%	74.9%	75.9%	77.2%
Prelim CBO Est. of Pres. Budget 3/2010					63.1%	68.7%	71.5%	72.6%	73.3%	74.3%	75.9%	77.6%	79.5%	81.8%	84.3%
Public	2006	2007	2008	2009	2010	2011	2012	2013	2014	2015	2016	2017	2018	2019	2020
CBO Est. of Pres. Budget 3/24/2010					63.2%	70.1%	73.6%	74.8%	75.7%	77.4%	79.6%	81.8%	84.3%	87.1%	90.0%
CBO Rev. Baseline 3/2010					61.7%	65.7%	67.0%	66.6%	65.9%	65.6%	65.8%	65.9%	66.2%	66.8%	67.5%
CBO Rev. Baseline 3/24/20 10					61.8%	65.8%	67.1%	66.6%	65.9%	65.7%	65.8%	66.0%	66.3%	66.9%	67.5%
Budget Resolution – S Budget 4/2010					62.1%	67.9%	70.7%	70.5%	70.0%	70.0%					
President's FY20 11					62.7%	69.6%	73.6%	74.6%	74.7%	75.9%	76.8%	77.4%	78.0%	78.9%	79.9%
Budget, MSR 7/2010															
CBO Rev. Baseline 8/2010					61.6%	66.1%	68.5%	68.4%	67.3%	67.3%	67.7%	68.1%	68.3%	68.8%	69.4%

Sources: CBO and OMB

Notes: OMB data are divided by OMB GDP estimates; CBO data by CBO GDP estimates. "CBO Rev. Baseline 3/20 10" data are taken from March 5, 2010, preliminary analysis. See source documents and text for additional caveats.

Table 11. Economic Projections: Gross Domestic Product (GDP) Billions of Current Dollars

Debt Held By The Public	FY 2006	FY 2007	FY 2008	FY 2009	FY 2010	FY 2011	FY 2012	FY 2013	FY 2014	FY 2015	FY 2016	FY 2017	FY 2018	FY 2019	FY 2020
OMB/Historical/ Actual	13,225	13,896	14,439	14,237	14,624	15,299	16,203	17,182	18,193	19,190	20,163	21,136	22,087	23,065	24,067
FY2009															
CBO Baseline, 1/2010				14,236	14,595	14,992	15,730	16,676	17,606	18,421	19,223	20,036	20,823	21,667	22,544
CBO Rev. Baseline 3/2010				14,236	14,595	14,992	15,730	16,676	17,606	18,421	19,223	20,036	20,823	21,667	22,544
CBO Rev. Baseline				14,236	14,595	14,992	15,730	16,676	17,606	18,421	19,223	20,036	20,823	21,667	22,544
3/24/20 10															
President's FY20 11 Budget,				14,230	14,666	15,148	15,764	16,705	17,760	18,630	19,508	20,398	21,293	22,205	23,154
MSR 7/2010															
CBO Rev. Baseline 8/2010				14,230	14,666	15,148	15,764	16,705	17,760	18,630	19,508	20,398	21,293	22,205	23,154

Sources: CBO and OMB

Notes: OMB data are divided by OMB GDP estimates; CBO data by CBO GDP estimates. "CBO Rev. Baseline 3/20 10" data are taken from March 5, 2010, preliminary analysis. See source documents and text for additional caveats.

Congress sets a ceiling on federal debt, which was raised twice in 2009 and once in early 2010. On February 17, 2009, the American Recovery and Reinvestment Act of 2009 (H.R. 1, P.L. 111- 5) increased the debt limit to $12,104 billion.[36]

The FY2010 budget resolution (S.Con.Res. 13) recommended policies that would lead to a debt subject to limit of $13,233 billion at the end of FY2010, a level that would require an increase in the statutory debt limit. The House's adoption of the conference report on the FY2010 budget resolution (S.Con.Res. 13) on April 29, 2009, triggered the automatic passage of H.J.Res. 45 to raise the debt limit to $13.029 trillion. In August 2009, Treasury reportedly said that the debt limit would be reached in mid-October, although it later stated that the limit would not be reached until mid or late December 2009. H.R. 4314, passed by the House on December 16, 2009, and by the Senate on December 24, raised the debt limit to $12.394 trillion when the President signed the measure (P.L. 111-123) on December 28. On January 28, the Senate passed an amended version of H.J.Res. 45, which the House passed on February 4 and the President signed on February 12 (P.L. 111-139), raising the federal debt limit to $14.294 trillion.

Federal debt held by the public rose sharply from 40.8% of GDP at the end of FY2008 to 53.0% at the end of FY2010.[37] That ratio, according to the August 2010 CBO baseline, is projected to rise to 66.1% at the end of FY2011. CBO's analysis of the President's FY2011 budget proposals suggests that ratio would reach 84.3% of GDP at the end of FY2020.

ECONOMIC PROJECTIONS AND ECONOMIC RECOVERY

Budget projections of the Administration and CBO are strongly influenced by expectations of the future health of the U.S. economy. The recent economic recession has also highlighted links between the federal budget and the economy. Budgetary projections for FY20 11 and beyond depend in large part on how robust economic recovery is expected to be. The timing and strength of the economic recovery from the current recession will likely have major effects on the federal budget. In particular, changes in the expected path of the U.S. economy would affect future revisions of CBO baseline estimates of federal outlays and revenues. On the one hand, a fasterthan-expected recovery would imply projections for higher federal revenues and lower outlays on certain "automatic stabilizer" programs whose spending increases when household incomes fall, which would lead to lower baseline projections of federal deficits. On the other hand, a slower or weaker-than-expected recovery would tend to increase projected federal deficits.

The current economic recession, as noted above, has been much deeper than many economic forecasters anticipated in 2007 and 2008. For instance, the U.S. economy contracted at an annualized real rate of 6.8% in the last quarter of 2008 and 4.9% in the first quarter of 2009, according to Commerce Department estimates, a sharper decline than many economists had expected. Estimates for the fourth quarter of 2009, which put annualized GDP growth at 5.0%, seemed to signal an end of the economic recession. [38] More recent economic data indicate a slow and uncertain period of economic recovery. According to Commerce Department estimates, the economy grew at an annualized real rate of 3.7% in the first quarter of 2010 and only 1.6% in the second quarter.[39] Given that in past years population growth has been about 1% per year, higher rates of economic growth would be necessary to reduce unemployment and raise living standards significantly.

Most economists expect unemployment rates to remain elevated for the medium term. Unemployment rates have remained at high levels, with the national unemployment rate standing at 9.5% in July 2010.[40] Unemployment rates are typically a lagging indicator, meaning that unemployment rates during recessions have stayed high even as other indicators of economic activity have showed signs of recovery. CBO estimates that the national unemployment rate will not recede to the 5% level until 2014.[41]

Many economic forecasters remain concerned about the medium-term strength of the economy for several reasons. State and local governments still face daunting fiscal problems, and many have exhausted rainy-day funds that cushioned them at the beginning of the recession. Interest- sensitive industries such as housing construction and automobile manufacturing that have helped spark past economic recoveries are considered unlikely to help economic recovery much in the near future. Many households are carrying high debt loads relative to historical levels and have suffered significant capital losses in housing and other investment, which may dampen private consumption for some time. Foreclosure rates are expected to continue at high levels, and concerns about the commercial real estate sector lead some to worry about the solvency of banks with substantial exposure to that sector. Finally, the financial services sector may face continuing challenges in coming years. For these reasons, many economists expect recovery from this recession to be more gradual than the economic rebound after shallower recessions in the past two decades. Forecasting turning points in economic trends, however, is difficult for technical and substantial reasons that are discussed in the next section. **Table 11** presents forecasts of gross domestic product (GDP), which measures the size of the economy.

ISSUES REGARDING BUDGET PROJECTIONS

Budget projections depend on models that reflect assumptions about the structure of the economy, expected tax and program changes, and how these interact, along with other factors that affect the budget. Changed economic conditions, such as faster or slower economic growth, higher or lower inflation, or new spending and tax policies, affect budget estimates and projections. In addition, technical components of the budget models may change as the structure of the economy evolves and as econometric techniques advance. In particular, major recessions can alter the structure of an economy in significant ways, making models based on historical data less reliable.

Budget forecasts, unlike most other types of economic forecasts, are constructed in order to estimate the incremental costs of policy changes (i.e., scoring) in a consistent manner. If policy changes do occur, actual budget outcomes will then differ from baseline estimates. Technical factors and changes in economic conditions also affect budget forecasts. In recent years, OMB and CBO have provided information about how past forecasts have varied from actual results.

CBO has analyzed the track record of its budget estimates extensively and now routinely includes information about its forecast record of baseline projections in its budget publications.[42] CBO also provides detailed explanations of why its projections differ from OMB projections.[43] CBO routinely provides a breakdown of economic, legislative, and technical factors responsible for divergences between past forecasts and actual outcomes.

Making accurate budget projections is inherently difficult. Reliable forecasting depends on the stability of trends. Some trends, such as population demographics, are highly predictable. For instance, many baby boomers will retire in the next decade, leading to higher spending for Medicare and Social Security. Estimating the growth in the beneficiary populations eligible for these programs is relatively straightforward. Budget estimates also depend on factors that are difficult to predict, such as future productivity growth and business cycles. Some factors that affect federal revenues, such as financial market trends, can be extremely volatile.

Making budget estimates and projections for the FY20 11 budget cycle is especially challenging for several reasons. The economy is starting to recover from a painful recession that differs from recent downturns in important ways. The economy could emerge from the recession transformed in ways that may take time to understand fully. Continuing turmoil in financial markets makes forecasting interest rates, which affect the costs of many federal programs and debt servicing, difficult. Forecasting economic recoveries, even for milder downturns, is difficult. The Obama Administration has proposed major program initiatives in many policy areas. Estimating the budgetary effects of major changes is more difficult than estimating effects of incremental changes.

Even in less tumultuous times, small changes in projected economic growth trajectories can lead to large budgetary consequences, especially for longer time horizons. Small changes in economic conditions, such as GDP growth, can produce large changes in the budget estimates. According to CBO estimates, a persistent 0.1% decrease in the real GDP growth rate would increase a deficit, including interest costs, by $61 billion cumulatively over a five-year period and by $273 billion over 10 years. Faster GDP growth would decrease deficits.[44]

Accuracy and Statistical Bias in Budget Forecasts

Budget projections are inherently uncertain. Two measures of the quality of economic forecasts are *statistical unbiasedness* and *accuracy*. Statistical unbiasedness means that average forecast errors over time are close to zero. An unbiased forecasting method may be of little use if forecast errors are large. Accuracy means that forecast errors are small, meaning that outcomes are close to predictions. Some forecasting methods may sacrifice unbiasedness in order to gain greater accuracy.[45] Most forecasters, as far as possible, strive to make projections that are both unbiased and accurate.

Presidential budget requests in recent years have included measures that can be used to assess the accuracy and statistical bias of previous forecasts.[46] Forecasts diverge from actual results because of legislative changes, unforeseen economic factors, and other factors. Current-law baseline projections will diverge from actual results when laws change, either expanding, constricting, or eliminating current programs, or by creating new programs. Projections that presume a president's policy proposals are enacted diverge from actual results if those policies are not enacted as proposed.

Since FY1982, OMB February deficit projections for the upcoming budget year underestimated the total deficit by $55 billion. Changes in legislation accounted for most of that divergence. The standard deviation of Administration budget year deficit/surplus estimates was $233 billion for the same period FY1982-FY2009.[47] A standard deviation measures the average size of forecast errors. The standard deviation for the corresponding four-years-ahead forecast was $343 billion. The accuracy of forecasts generally declines as the forecast window extends to later years because more policy and economic changes can occur in the interim.

OMB used its standard deviation estimate to compute upper and lower bounds for deficit projections.[48] In the FY20 11 budget submission, OMB estimated the FY20 15 federal deficit would be 3.9% of GDP, with an upper bound of 10.4% of GDP and a lower bound of a 2.6% surplus.[49] If the statistical assumptions underlying that calculation were valid, the actual FY20 15 deficit should fall within the upper and lower bounds with a 90% probability. The spread between the upper and lower bounds indicates the estimated precision of the five-years-ahead deficit forecast.

End Notes

[1] The Budget and Accounting Act of 1921 requires the President to submit a budget to Congress each year. Current law (31 U.S.C. 1105(a)) requires the President to submit a budget no earlier than the first Monday in January, and no later than the first Monday in February.

[2] For an overview of federal budgetary issues, see CRS Report R41097, *The FY2011 Federal Budget*, by Mindy R. Levit.

[3] U.S. Department of Commerce, Bureau of Economic Analysis, "Gross Domestic Product: Second Quarter 2010 (2nd Estimate)," press release BEA 10-41, August 27, 2010, available at http://www.bea.gov/newsreleases/national/gdp/ 2010/pdf/gdp2q10_2nd.pdf.

[4] Ibid.

[5] Testimony of Benjamin S. Bernanke, Chairman of the Federal Reserve Board, in U.S. Congress, Senate Committee on Banking, Housing, and Urban Affairs, "Semiannual Monetary Policy Report to the Congress," hearings, 111th Cong., 2nd sess., July 21, 2010, available at http://www.federalreserve.gov/newsevents/testimony/ bernanke20100721a.htm.

[6] U.S. Department of Labor, Bureau of Labor Statistics, "The Employment Situation: July 2010," press release USDL10-1076, August 6, 2010, available at *http://www.bls.gov/new s.release/pdf/empsit.pdf.*

[7] U.S. Congressional Budget Office, *The Budget and Economic Outlook: An Update*, August 19, 2010, p. 1, available at http://www.cbo.gov/doc.cfm?index=11705.

[8] U.S. Congressional Budget Office, *The Budget and Economic Outlook: An Update*, August 19, 2010, Table 1-2, available at http://www.cbo.gov/doc.cfm?index=11705.

[9] The Obama Administration's FY20 11 budget submission materials are available at http://www.whitehouse.gov/omb/ budget/.

[10] White House, "National Commission on Fiscal Responsibility and Reform," Executive Order 13531, February 18, 2010, 75 Federal Register 7927, February 23, 2010, available at http://edocket.access

[11] See CRS Report RL3 1443, *The "Deeming Resolution": A Budget Enforcement Tool*, by Robert Keith. For one interpretation of the budgetary implications of H.Res. 1493, see U.S. Senate Budget Committee (Minority), "Budget Perspective: The House 'Enforcement Resolution,'" press release, July 14, 2010, available at http://budget.senate.gov/ republican/pressarchive/2010-07-14BudgetPerspective.pdf.

[12] CBO's role is set forth in Title II of the Congressional Budget and Impoundment Control Act of 1974 (P.L. 93-344) and the Balanced Budget and Emergency Deficit Control Act of 1985 (P.L. 99-177). While the portions of that legislation affecting the CBO current-law baseline expired in September 2006, CBO has not changed how it constructs baseline projections.

[13] See CRS Report R41 111, *Expiration and Extension of the Individual Income Tax Cuts First Enacted in 2001 and 2003: Background and Analysis*, by Maxim Shvedov.

[14] The American Recovery and Reinvestment Act of 2009 (P.L. 111-5) included a one-year patch for the 2009 tax year. For details, see CRS Report RL30 149, *The Alternative Minimum Tax for Individuals*, by Steven Maguire.

[15] For details, see CRS Report RS22915, Temporary Extension of Unemployment Benefits: Emergency Unemployment Compensation (EUC08), by Katelin P. Isaacs, Julie M. Whittaker, and Alison M. Shelton.

[16] For details, see CRS Report R40907, Medicare Physician Payment Updates and the Sustainable Growth Rate (SGR) System, by Jim Hahn.

[17] U.S. Congress, Joint Committee on Taxation, "Estimated Revenue Effects Of The Revenue Provisions Contained In The President's Fiscal Year 2011 Budget," JCX-7-10, March 8, 2010.

[18] U.S. Congress, Congressional Budget Office, The Long-term Budget Outlook, June 2009, available at http://www.cbo.gov/doc.cfm?index=10297&zzz=39116.

[19] U.S. Congress, Congressional Budget Office, The Budget and Economic Outlook: Fiscal Years 2010 to 2020, January 2010, available at http://www.cbo.gov/ftpdocs/108xx/doc10871/01-26-Outlook.pdf. CBO calls totals for the current fiscal year "estimates" and calls totals for future years "projections."

[20] Ibid., Table 1-5.

[21] U.S. Congress, Congressional Budget Office, A Preliminary Analysis of the President's Budget Request for 2011, letter to the Honorable Daniel K. Inouye dated March 5, 2010, available at http://www.cbo.gov/ftpdocs/112xx/doc11231/index.cfm. Also see Douglas Elmendorf, "Preliminary Analysis of the President's Budget," CBO Director's blog, available at http://cboblog.cbo.gov/?p=482.

[22] U.S. Congress, Congressional Budget Office, An Analysis of the President's Budgetary Proposals for Fiscal Year 2011, March 24, 2009, available at *http://www.cbo.gov/ftpdocs/1* 12xx/doc11280/03-24-apb.pdf.

[23] CRS Report R40444, State Children's Health Insurance Program (CHIP): A Brief Overview, by Elicia J. Herz, Chris L. Peterson, and Evelyne P. Baumrucker.

[24] Expired budget authority is kept on the federal government's books for five years. After five years, balances are cancelled and expired accounts are closed. For a detailed description of federal appropriations procedures, see U.S. Government Accountability Office, *Principles of Federal Appropriations Law* (known as the "Red Book"), vol. 1, GAO-04-261 SP, January 2004, available at http://www.gao.gov/legal/redbook.html.

[25] For details, see CRS Report RL34424, *Trends in Discretionary Spending*, by D. Andrew Austin and Mindy R. Levit.

[26] U.S. Congressional Budget Office, *The Budget and Economic Outlook: An Update*, August 19, 2010, available at http://www.cbo.gov/doc.cfm?index=11705.

[27] See notes for Office of Management and Budget, *Budget of the U.S. Government*, Table S-11, available at http://www.whitehouse.gov/omb/budget/fy2011/assets. The George W. Bush Administration used a different definition for "security" funding.

[28] For details, see CRS Report R41 127, *The SAFRA Act: Education Programs in the FY2010 Budget Reconciliation* , coordinated by Cassandria Dortch.

[29] For details, see CRS Report RL33074, *Mandatory Spending Since 1962*, by D. Andrew Austin and Mindy R. Levit.

[30] Very small surpluses might not reduce debt held by the public in some circumstances. In recent years, major financial interventions, such as the conservatorships of Fannie Mae and Freddie Mac, have led to increases in federal indebtedness that do not match federal deficits.

[31] See CRS Report RL33657, *Running Deficits: Positives and Pitfalls*, by D. Andrew Austin.

[32] U.S. Congress, Congressional Budget Office, *The Long-Term Budget Outlook*, June 2009, available at http://www.cbo.gov/doc.cfm?index=10297.

[33] Gross federal debt is also referred to as total debt or total public debt outstanding. Intragovernmental debt is also referred to as intragovernmental holdings or debt held by federal government accounts.

[34] U.S. Executive Office of the President, Office of Management and Budget, *Budget of the U.S. Government, Fiscal Year 2009, Analytical Perspectives*, February 2008, p. 408.

[35] Eric M. Patashinik, *Putting Trust in the U.S. Budget: Federal Trust Funds and the Politics of Commitment* (Cambridge, UK: Cambridge, 2000).

[36] See CRS Report RL31967, *The Debt Limit: History and Recent Increases*, by D. Andrew Austin and Mindy R. Levit.

[37] U.S. Congress, Congressional Budget Office, *The Budget and Economic Outlook: Fiscal Years 2010 to 2020*, January 2010, available at http://www.cbo.gov/ftpdocs/108xx/doc10871/01-26-Outlook.pdf.

[38] U.S. Department of Commerce, Bureau of Economic Analysis, "Gross Domestic Product: Second Quarter 2010 (2nd Estimate)," press release BEA 10-41, August 27, 2010, available at http://www.bea.gov/newsreleases/national/gdp/ 2010/pdf/gdp2q10_2nd.pdf.

[39] Ibid.

[40] U.S. Department of Labor, Bureau of Labor Statistics, "The Employment Situation: July 2010," press release USDL10-1076, August 6, 2010, available at http://www.bls.gov/ news.release/pdf/empsit.pdf.

[41] U.S. Congressional Budget Office, *The Budget and Economic Outlook: An Update*, August 19, 2010, p. 1, available at http://www.cbo.gov/doc.cfm?index=11705.

[42] U.S. Congress, Congressional Budget Office, "The Uncertainty of Budget Projections: A Discussion of Data and Methods," March 2006.

[43] U.S. Congress, Congressional Budget Office, "*Comparing Budget and Accounting Measures of the Federal Government's Fiscal Condition*," December 2006.

[44] Slower economic growth would also reduce a budget surplus.

[45] There may be a tradeoff between statistical unbiasedness and accuracy because some statistically biased methods may generate forecasts with greater accuracy. Also, other properties of forecasts may be important, such as predicting turning points in economic trends. For a nontechnical discussion of economic forecasting, see Peter Kennedy, *A Guide to Econometrics*, 3rd ed., Boston: MIT Press, 1992, ch. 17, pp. 268-277.

[46] Office of Management and Budget, *Budget of the U.S. Government: Analytical Perspectives, FY2011,* ch. 29, "Comparison of Actual to Estimated Totals," available at *http://www.whitehouse.gov/omb/budget/fy2011/assets* technical_analyses.pdf.

[47] CRS calculation based on OMB data.

[48] The upper and lower bounds were computed assuming that forecast errors for different years are statistically independent and are normally distributed.

[49] Office of Management and Budget, *Budget of the U.S. Government: Analytical Perspectives, FY2011,"* ch. 3, "Interactions between the Economy and the Budget," p. 23, available at http://www.whitehouse.gov/omb/budget/ fy20 1 1/assets/econ_analyses.pdf.

CHAPTER SOURCES

The following chapters have been previously published:

Chapter 1 – This is an edited, excerpted and augmented edition of a United States Congressional Research Service publication, Report Order Code 98-721, dated December 2, 2010.

Chapter 2 – This is an edited, excerpted and augmented edition of a United States Congressional Research Service publication, Report Order Code 97-865, dated December 1, 2010.

Chapter 3 – This is an edited, excerpted and augmented edition of a United States Congressional Research Service publication, Report Order Code 98-560, dated December 1, 2010.

Chapter 4 – This is an edited, excerpted and augmented edition of a United States Congressional Research Service publication, Report Order Code RS20144, dated November 29, 2010.

Chapter 5 – This is an edited, excerpted and augmented edition of a United States Congressional Research Service publication, Report Order Code RS20129, dated December 1, 2010.

Chapter 6 – This is an edited, excerpted and augmented edition of a United States Congressional Research Service publication, Report Order Code 98-410, dated November 29, 2010.

Chapter 7 – This is an edited, excerpted and augmented edition of a United States Congressional Research Service publication, Report Order Code R40113, dated September 2, 2010.

Chapter 8 – This is an edited, excerpted and augmented edition of a United States Congressional Research Service publication, Report Order Code R41097, dated August 4, 2010.

Chapter 9 – This is an edited, excerpted and augmented edition of a United States Congressional Research Service publication, Report Order Code R41147, dated September 1, 2010.

INDEX

R

S